USING ETHNOGRAPHIC DATA

ETHNOGRAPHER'S TOOLKIT

Edited by Jean J. Schensul, *Institute for Community Research, Hartford*, and
Margaret D. LeCompte, *School of Education, University of Colorado, Boulder*

The **Ethnographer's Toolkit** is designed with you, the novice fieldworker, in mind. In a series of seven brief books, the editors and authors of the **Toolkit** take you through the multiple, complex steps of doing ethnographic research in simple, reader-friendly language. Case studies, checklists, key points to remember, and additional resources to consult, are all included to help the reader fully understand the ethnographic process. Eschewing a step-by-step formula approach, the authors are able to explain the complicated tasks and relationships that occur in the field in clear, helpful ways. Research designs, data collection techniques, analytical strategies, research collaborations, and an array of uses for ethnographic work in policy, programming, and practice, are described in these volumes. The **Toolkit** is the perfect starting point for professionals in diverse professional fields including social welfare, education, health, economic development, and the arts, as well as for advanced students and experienced researchers unfamiliar with the demands of conducting good ethnography.

Summer 1999/ 7 volumes/ paperback boxed set/ 0-7619-9042-9

BOOKS IN THE ETHNOGRAPHER'S TOOLKIT

1. **Designing and Conducting Ethnographic Research** by Margaret D. LeCompte and Jean J. Schensul, 0-7619-8975-7 (paperback)
2. **Essential Ethnographic Methods: Observations, Interviews, and Questionnaires** by Stephen Schensul, Jean J. Schensul, and Margaret D. LeCompte, 0-7619-9144-1 (paperback)
3. **Enhanced Ethnographic Methods: Audiovisual Techniques, Focused Group Interviews, and Elicitation Techniques** by Jean J. Schensul, Margaret D. LeCompte, Bonnie K. Nastasi, and Stephen P. Borgatti, 0-7619-9129-8 (paperback)
4. **Mapping Social Networks, Spatial Data, and Hidden Populations** by Jean J. Schensul, Margaret D. LeCompte, Robert T. Trotter II, Ellen K. Cromley, and Merrill Singer, 0-7619-9112-3 (paperback)
5. **Analyzing and Interpreting Ethnographic Data** by Margaret D. LeCompte and Jean J. Schensul, 0-7619-8974-9 (paperback)
6. **Researcher Roles and Research Partnerships** by Margaret D. LeCompte, Jean J. Schensul, Margaret R. Weeks, and Merrill Singer, 0-7619-8973-0 (paperback)
7. **Using Ethnographic Data: Interventions, Public Programming, and Public Policy,** by Jean J. Schensul, Margaret D. LeCompte, G. Alfred Hess, Jr., Bonnie K. Nastasi, Marlene J. Berg, Lynne Williamson, Jeremy Brecher, and Ruth Glasser, 0-7619-8972-2 (paperback)

USING ETHNOGRAPHIC DATA

Interventions, Public Programming, and Public Policy

JEAN J. SCHENSUL
MARGARET D. LeCOMPTE
G. ALFRED HESS, JR.
BONNIE K. NASTASI
MARLENE J. BERG
LYNNE WILLIAMSON
JEREMY BRECHER
RUTH GLASSER

7 ETHNOGRAPHER'S TOOLKIT

ALTAMIRA PRESS
A Division of Sage Publications, Inc.
Walnut Creek ◆ London ◆ New Delhi

INTRODUCTION

The **Ethnographer's Toolkit** is a series of texts on how to plan, design, carry out, and use the results of applied ethnographic research. Ethnography, as an approach to research, may be unfamiliar to people accustomed to more traditional forms of research, but we believe that applied ethnography will prove not only congenial but essential to both researchers and practitioners. Many kinds of evaluative or investigative questions that arise in the course of program planning and implementation cannot really be answered very well with standard research methods, such as experiments or collection of quantifiable data, alone. Often, there are not any data yet to quantify nor programs whose effectiveness needs to be assessed! Sometimes, the research problem to be addressed is not yet clearly identified and must be discovered. In such cases, ethnographic research provides a valid and important way to find out what *is* happening in programs and to help practitioners plan their activities.

This book series defines what ethnographic research is, when it should be used, and how it can be used to identify and solve complex social problems, especially those not readily amenable to traditional quantitative or experimental research methods alone. It is designed for educators; service professionals; professors of applied students in the fields of teaching, social and health services, communications, engineering, and business; and students working in applied field settings.

Ethnography is a peculiarly human endeavor. Many of its practitioners have commented that, unlike other approaches to research, the researcher is the primary tool for collecting primary data. That is, as Books 1, 2, 3, and 4 demonstrate, the ethnographer's principal database is amassed in the course of human interaction: direct observation; face-to-face interviewing and elicitation; audiovisual recording; and mapping the networks, times, and places in which human interactions occur. Thus, as Book 6 makes clear, the personal characteristics and activities of researchers as human beings and as scientists become salient in ways not applicable in research where the investigator maintains more distance from the people and phenomena under study.

Book 1 of the **Ethnographer's Toolkit**, *Designing and Conducting Ethnographic Research,* defines what ethnographic research is and the predominant viewpoints or paradigms that guide ethnography. It provides the reader with an overview of research methods and design, including how to develop research questions, what to consider in setting up the mechanics of a research project, and how to devise a sampling plan. Ways of collecting and analyzing data, as well as ethical considerations in ethnography conclude this overall introduction to the series. In Book 2 of the **Ethnographer's Toolkit,** titled *Essential Ethnographic Methods,* readers are provided with an introduction to participant and nonparticipant observation, interviewing, and ethnographically informed survey research, including systematically administered structured interviews and questionnaires. These data collection strategies are fundamental to good ethnographic research. The essential methods provide ethnographers with tools to answer the principal ethnographic questions: "What's happening in this setting?" "Who is engaging in what kind of activities?" and "Why are they doing what they are doing?" Ethnographers use these tools to enter a field situation to obtain basic information about social structure, social events, cultural patterns, and the meanings people give to these patterns. The essential tools also permit ethnographers to learn about new situations from the perspective of insiders because they require ethnographers to become involved in the local cultural setting and to acquire their knowledge through hands-on experience.

In Book 3, *Enhanced Ethnographic Methods,* the reader adds to this basic inventory of ethnographic tools three different but important approaches to data collection, each one a complement to the essential methods presented in Book 2. These tools are audiovisual techniques, focused group interviews, and elicitation techniques. We have termed these data collection strategies "enhanced ethnographic methods" because each of them parallels and enhances a strategy first presented in Book 2.

Audiovisual techniques, which involve recording behavior and speech using electronic equipment, expand the capacity of ethnographers to observe and listen by creating a more complete and permanent record of events and speech. Focused group interviews permit ethnographers to interview more than one person at a time. Finally, elicitation techniques allow ethnographers to quantify qualitative or perceptual data on how individuals and groups of people think about and organize perceptions of their cultural world.

It is important for the reader to recognize that whereas the essential ethnographic methods described in Book 2 can be used alone, the enhanced ethnographic methods covered in Book 3 cannot, by themselves, provide a fully rounded picture of cultural life in a community, organization, work group, school, or other setting. Instead, they must be used in combination with the essential methods outlined in Book 2. Doing so adds dimensions of depth and accuracy to the cultural portrait constructed by the ethnographer.

In Book 4, *Mapping Social Networks, Spatial Data, and Hidden Populations,* we add to the enhanced methods of data collection and analysis used by ethnographers. However, the approach taken in Book 4 is informed by a somewhat different perspective on the way social life is organized in communities. Whereas the previous books focus primarily on ways of understanding cultural patterns and the interactions of individuals and groups in cultural settings, Book 4 focuses on social networks; social arrangements in "sociogeographic space"; and approaches to seeking, identifying, and recruiting hidden populations. The methods outlined in the three chapters of this book—"Friends, Relatives, and Relevant Others: Conducting Ethnographic Network Studies," "Mapping Spatial Data," and "Studying Hidden Populations"—are intended to help researchers to see communities as connections among individuals, among agencies, between individuals and agencies, and as sites where hidden behavior can be studied with proper attention to approach and confidentiality.

Book 5, *Analyzing and Interpreting Ethnographic Data,* provides the reader with a variety of methods for transforming piles of fieldnotes, observations, audio- and videotapes, questionnaires, surveys, documents, maps, and other kinds of data into research results that help people to understand their world more fully and facilitate problem solving. Addressing both narrative and qualitative, as well as quantitative—or enumerated—data, Book 5 discusses methods for organizing, retrieving, rendering manageable, and interpreting the data collected in ethnographic research.

In Book 6, *Researcher Roles and Research Partnerships,* we discuss the special requirements that doing ethnographic research imposes on its practitioners. Throughout the **Ethnographer's Toolkit** series, we have argued that there is little difference between the exercise of ethnography as a systematic and scientific enterprise, and applied ethnography as that same systematic and scientific enterprise used specifically for helping people identify and solve human problems. To that end, in Chapter 1, "Researcher Roles," we first describe how the work of ethnographers is inextricably tied to the type of person the ethnographer is, the particular social and cultural context of the research site, and the tasks and responsibilities that ethnographers assume in the field.

In the second chapter, "Building Research Partnerships," we recognize that ethnography is seldom done by lone researchers by discussing how ethnographers assemble research teams, establish partnerships with individuals and institutions in the field, and work collaboratively with a wide range of people and organizations to solve mutually identified problems. The chapter explores three types of research partnerships: ethnographic research teams, interdisciplinary teams, and action research partnerships. For each, ethical and procedural considerations, including developing social and managerial infrastructure, establishing and breaking contracts, negotiating different organizational cultures and values, and resolving conflicts, are reviewed.

This book, the last in the **Ethnographer's Toolkit,** titled *Using Ethnographic Data: Interventions, Public Programmimg, and Public Policy,* consists of three chapters that present general guidelines and case studies demonstrating how ethnographers have used ethnographic data in planning public programs, evaluating and developing interventions, and influencing public policy.

Chapter 1 focuses on the uses of ethnography in program development and evaluation. Authors Bonnie Nastasi and Marlene Berg, writing from an education and prevention perspective, take a comprehensive and interactive view of programming, defining it as the implementation of a program from conceptualization to outcome evaluation. Ethnographic research interacts with program activities during planning, implementation, and process and outcome evaluation. The interaction of research with program activities contributes to culturally and situationally appropriate programs, as well as to program improvement and staff training. They show through U.S.-based and international examples how ethnography can explain program outcomes while also producing substantive knowledge and generating new theory.

Chapter 2 addresses the challenge of using ethnography to inform policy. Alfred Hess, an experienced educational anthropologist, provides examples from his work with the Chicago Panel, an agency established to assist the Chicago Public Schools to move forward with decentralized management and school reform. He notes that it is not enough for ethnographers to make policy recommendations. Instead, it is critical to position oneself to be able both to conduct research and understand the situations in which policy decisions are made. Without understanding both the culture of the research setting—in this case, schools—and the culture of policy making, it becomes challenging, if not impossible, to influence policymakers directly. The chapter provides a detailed description of tools that ethnographers can use to influence policy based on the results of their research, as well as suggestions for how to use these tools effectively.

The book series concludes with a final chapter on using ethnography to influence public programming. The authors, who are public historians, folklorists, and anthropologists, use the term *public programming* to refer to programs and projects that are designed to inform broad public audiences about the history, material and expressive culture, folklore, and daily life of communities. Consistent with the philosophy of the overall series, they take the position that public programming should be based on careful ethnographic and ethnohistorical fieldwork. To address directly the issue of cultural rights and control over representation, they provide examples of how fieldwork is conducted in partnership with those whose cultures are to be represented in galleries, museums, and performance series; on radio and television; and through videos, CD recordings, and the Internet. Through three case histories, they show readers how to choose fieldwork methods that respect reciprocity and lead to deepened community, as well as ethnographers', understanding of community cultural representation. The chapter highlights for readers ways of addressing some of the central challenges in building research and representation partnerships with culturally and linguistically diverse communities at various points in the evolution of their desire to portray their presence and their culture to the broader public. The chapter is a fitting conclusion to the series, which emphasizes throughout the central importance of relationship in ethnographic engagement.

—Jean J. Schensul and Margaret D. LeCompte

1

USING ETHNOGRAPHY TO STRENGTHEN AND EVALUATE INTERVENTION PROGRAMS

Bonnie K. Nastasi
Marlene J. Berg

INTRODUCTION

The purpose of this chapter is to help **program developers**—people who conduct interventions for the purpose of bringing about individual, organizational, or community change—and **program evaluators**—people who measure the effectiveness of intervention programs—to use ethnography to improve the quality of their programs. Books 2, 3, and 4 provide guidelines and examples designed to assist programmers in selecting and using ethnographic methods for collecting data that inform the design, implementation, and evaluation of such programs. Here, we discuss and provide examples of ways in which these tools can be used in program assessment. **Programs**

Definition: Program developers (programmers) are those who create and conduct interventions to bring about change in individuals, groups, organizations, or communities

AUTHORS' NOTE: Gratitude is expressed to the series editors for their valuable comments on earlier versions of this chapter.

Definition: Program evaluators are people who measure the effectiveness of intervention programs

Definition: A program is an intervention or strategy intended to bring about change in individuals, groups, institutions, or communities

Cross Reference: See Book 1, Chapter 3 for a discussion of ecological and other paradigms guiding research and intervention

may focus on educational, psychological, organizational, social, or cultural change. The examples we cite in this chapter come mainly from work in two community-based projects in Hartford, Connecticut and Kandy, Sri Lanka. These programs use an **ecological approach**, addressing change at the individual, group, system, and community levels. The general theories of change guiding these programs have been modified through ethnographic research to be context specific. That is what ethnography can contribute most effectively—a better understanding of the local conditions, culture, meaning, and facilitators and barriers to carrying out the program successfully. At the same time, these two examples illustrate general issues in using ethnographic methods and results to inform, improve, and evaluate programs. We begin by describing the process of developing intervention programs.

THE PROCESS OF DEVELOPING INTERVENTION PROGRAMS

Definition: Program development is the process of designing, carrying out, and evaluating a program

We use the term **program development** in this chapter to refer to the entire process of designing, implementing, and evaluating intervention programs from beginning to end. Ideally, this is an integrated process with coordination across the three phases of design, implementation, and evaluation. In an integrated process, there are direct links between program goals, which are determined during the design phase; program activities or intervention strategies which are carried out during the implementation phase; and evaluation strategies. There also is ongoing communication between designers, interventionists, and evaluators. In practice, two or even all three roles may be performed by the same team, or they may be carried out by different people who enter a project at different stages and points in time.

Consistent with the ethnographer's recognition of the importance of program participants' perspectives at all stages of development, programming ideally should include continuous and well-thought-out involvement of **key stakeholders** (e.g., program recipients, staff who implement the program, and community representatives). Finally, ideal program development should involve an iterative process of data collection and program development. By this we mean that data collected during each program phase should influence decision making specific to both that phase and other phases. For example, data collected during implementation of a classroom-based social skills training program can lead not only to further staff training in the use of role playing with children who have language difficulties, but also to revision of the program objectives and curriculum to include sessions on verbal and nonverbal communication if they are needed.

Definition: Key stakeholders are all those who have a vested interest in the program and its outcomes

We recognize, however, that not all ethnographers enter a program planning process at the beginning or are able to carry it through to the end. Some researchers conduct only **formative research**—for example, they may collect information on children's experiences and perceptions of violence that contribute to the development of curriculum materials. Or they may assess the ways in which children learn at home and at school with the hope of increasing compatibility between the two. Others may be asked to conduct a documentation of the way a program is being carried out in line with its goals and objectives, or its management plan, without ever having been involved in conceptualizing it. Finally, ethnographers have sometimes been hired to help explain quantitative evaluation results in greater detail, or even, in case studies, to describe program results after the fact. We have tried to consider the role of ethnography in each of these phases of program development, both separately and as part of an integrated process. Finally, we consider the use of ethnography within partici-

Definition: Formative research is research that is carried out before a program is finalized and that contributes to its development

patory programs (i.e., where stakeholders participate with programmers in decision making) and nonparticipatory programs (i.e., where programmers make decisions either independently or on behalf of stakeholders).

Phases of Program Development

The three phases of program development are the following:

- Program Design or Planning
- Implementation
- Evaluation

Cross Reference: See Book 1, Chapter 4, for an overview of research design, and Book 1, Chapters 5, 6, and 7, for other aspects of research design

Program design or planning—typically the first phase of program development—is focused on identifying needs and resources, determining program goals and objectives, and identifying procedures for program implementation and evaluation. If research design is the plan for conducting the research from beginning to end, program design is the plan for conducting a program from start to finish. Both require modifications along the way based on experience and additional data collection.

Program implementation involves the numerous activities that are carried out in order to make the program work "on the ground":

- Hiring and training staff
- Recruiting participants
- Developing intervention activities
- Conducting intervention sessions

Program evaluation involves data collection to answer the following questions:

- Were intervention sessions or activities carried out as planned?
- What was actually being done in the program?

- What did the program look like as implemented?
- How effective was the intervention?
- Were program objectives met?
- How acceptable was the intervention to participants?
- Were program recipients and implementers pleased with the process and outcomes?
- Were they comfortable engaging in activities?

Why Collect Data for Program Development?

Data collection can have many purposes in program development, depending on the phase and the needs of programmers for additional information about the setting or the groups for whom the program is intended. *Program planners* collect data in order to do the following:

- Better understand the target problem. For example, what kinds of drugs are adolescents using or abusing? What factors contribute to substance abuse by youth?
- Determine the need for intervention in the target population. For example, how widespread is adolescent substance abuse? How seriously is it viewed in the community? How available are substance abuse prevention programs in the community?
- Identify available resources. For example, what staff and funding are available in the community?
- Ensure that interventions are culture specific, reflecting norms, language, and practices of the target population

Interventionists collect data during program implementation in order to do the following:

- Monitor the program's development and process
- Understand what staff are doing to deliver the program
- Determine changes in target behaviors related to the intervention
- Modify the program
- Identify staff training needs

Program evaluators collect data in order to do the following:

- Examine the acceptability of the program to its staff and recipients—whether the program is feasible and whether it is perceived to be appropriate and useful
- Assess "program integrity"—whether the program is being delivered as intended or in some other way
- Monitor the effectiveness of the intervention—what changes occurred during the delivery of the program and whether they affected the direction of program goals
- Evaluate intervention outcomes—to what extent were goals met?

Cross Reference: See Books 2, Chapters 2 and 3, for more information on how to build and extend theory with ethnographic data

Data collected across all phases can be used to build or extend theory as well. For example, data collected during the program planning stage can help to build culture-specific theory to guide the program by identifying cultural factors such as familial and community drinking practices that influence the target phenomenon, which, in this case, is substance abuse by adolescents. Data on these topics that are collected while the program is going on can further extend the theoretical framework and improve it for the next phase of the program or for use with other programs in the future. Alternatively, data about the links between program outcomes and specific intervention strategies may extend our knowledge of effective interventions. Many different kinds of data can be collected to serve these purposes.

Ethnographic Techniques

Ethnographic techniques can be used across the various phases of program development (see Table 1.1). Selection and specific use of the techniques depends on the purpose, as our examples illustrate. The same techniques can be used to serve multiple purposes. For example, videotaped observations can be used both to document program implementation and facilitate staff training. We provide only a brief review of each technique. More in-depth discussion of these techniques can be found in other books in this series (see also Bernard, 1995, 1998; Krueger, 1994; LeCompte, Millroy, & Preissle, 1992; Lincoln & Guba, 1985; Miles & Huberman, 1994; Pelto & Pelto, 1978; Spradley, 1979, 1980).

Cross Reference:
See Books 2, 3, and 4 for details on ethnographic techniques

Key informant interviews. Key informant interviews are designed to gather data from individuals who are believed to hold key positions within the culture (e.g., knowledgeable representatives of key stakeholder groups). This type of interview is typically informal and unstructured, and it provides the researcher or program planner with the opportunity to gain information about the culture that is relevant to the target phenomenon. Key informants can be interviewed individually or in groups. For example, prior to formal data collection in a community, one might conduct informal interviews with a community health worker about the sexual concerns of young women. The worker would be asked to comment on the topic based on his or her ongoing contacts with families. Alternatively, the program planner might visit a local basketball court to talk with adolescent males about the facilitators and barriers to the use of school computers and other desired resources.

Cross Reference:
See Book 2, Chapters 4 and 6, for more information on how to conduct in-depth interviews with key informants

In-depth interviewing. In-depth interviewing is a more systematic approach to data collection. Typically conducted with individuals, these interviews focus on gathering detailed information about specific topics across a sample. Interviewees are selected purposefully or at random to represent a particular population. For example, to thoroughly understand factors that affect school reform, researchers could conduct in-depth interviews with representative youth about their social networks, attitudes toward education, daily schedules, expectations of teacher performance, sources of information and education, and their personal educational histories.

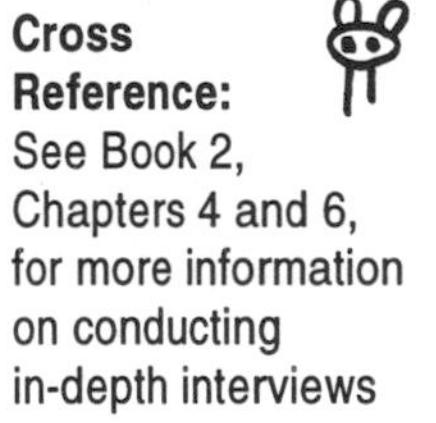

Cross Reference:
See Book 2, Chapters 4 and 6, for more information on conducting in-depth interviews

TABLE 1.1 Application of Ethnographic Methods in the Phases of Program Development

Ethnographic Methods	*Program Design*	*Program Implementation*	*Program Evaluation*
Key informant interviews	Identify perceived needs and existing resources Identify key stakeholders	Monitor program implementation Identify need for further training and program modification Monitor program acceptability	Document perceived outcomes Assess program acceptability Examine individual or cultural changes in contexts external to the intervention (e.g., community-related changes) Institutionalization and sustainability of intervention
In-depth interviews	Identify concerns Identify key cultural and individual factors related to concerns Gather real-life examples of problem situations and current repertoire of skills and resources	Monitor program implementation Identify need for further training and program modification Monitor program acceptability	Document perceived outcomes Assess program acceptability Examine individual or cultural changes in contexts external to the intervention (e.g., community-related changes) Examine institutionalization and sustainability of intervention
Focus groups	Identify perceived needs Develop program model Establish program goals Inform program content Establish partnership Promote program acceptability	Monitor program implementation Identify need for further training and program modification Monitor program acceptability	Document perceived outcomes Assess program acceptability Examine individual or cultural changes in contexts external to the intervention (e.g., community-related changes) Examine institutionalization and sustainability of intervention
Naturalistic observation	Identify problems and existing resources Gather real-life examples of problem situations and current repertoire of skills and resources	Document program implementation Identify need for additional staff training and program modification	Document changes in target behaviors in real-life settings Document unexpected effects on larger context (e.g., community norms) Examine institutionalization and sustainability of intervention Document program integrity

Ethnographic Methods	*Program Design*	*Program Implementation*	*Program Evaluation*
Logs/journals/ narratives	Establish baseline measure of problems and related factors Gather real-life examples of problem situations and current repertoire of skills and resources	Document program implementation Monitor program acceptability Identify need for additional staff training and program modification	Document perceived outcomes Examine generalization (e.g., use of new skills in other settings) and maintenance (extended use of new skills) of program outcomes Examine program acceptability Assess program integrity
Curriculum-based/ artifacts	Gather information about existing resources Identify and examine previous intervention efforts	Document program implementation Document the dynamics of change in the intervention context Identify need for program modification	Evaluate program impact on session-by-session basis Document the process of change in target skills, beliefs, etc. Provide additional data about the target constructs to inform theory Assess program integrity
Ethnographic surveys	Establish baseline measure of prevalence regarding identified problem and related factors Preintervention measure of target skills, beliefs, behaviors, etc.		Evaluate program effects/ outcomes Prepost intervention measure of target skills, beliefs, behaviors, etc. Examine pre-post intervention changes Examine generalization and maintenance (through follow-up surveys)
Pilesorts	Formulate definitions of key constructs	Intervention activity to promote understanding of individual and collective meaning of key constructs	Examine changes in definitions of key constructs (program outcomes)

Focus groups. Focus groups are a variation of interviews designed for the purpose of gathering data about a specific (focused) topic from a group of individuals (Krueger, 1994; Morgan, 1988; Morgan & Krueger, 1998; Schensul, 1999). As with in-depth interviews, focus group participants are selected purposefully or at random to represent certain

Cross Reference: See Book 3, Chapter 2, on focused group interviews

populations. Group members are asked to comment on specific topics individually and as a group as representative of their peers. Focus group members may be asked to discuss the topic and reach a consensus of opinion. Focus groups might be used in program development to gather information from community members about specific programming needs or to examine their perceptions about the acceptability of proposed interventions. For example, before designing school-based mental health programs, Nastasi and her colleagues (Nastasi, Varjas, Sarkar, & Jayasena, 1998) conducted focus groups with students and teachers to identify specific mental health needs of youth.

Cross Reference: See Book 2, Chapters 4 and 5, on participant unstructured and semistructured observations, and Book 3, Chapter 1, for methods of structured observation using audio-visual recording techniques

Naturalistic observations. Naturalistic observations are conducted in real-life contexts for the purpose of recording natural occurrences relevant to the specific intervention. They can range from participative (participant observation) to fully structured and nonparticipative. Observations may be recorded via fieldnotes, which provide narrative descriptions, or with the use of videotape recorders, which provide permanent audiovisual records. Observations can focus on individual and contextual factors (e.g., by recording students' behaviors and instructional methods in a classroom). During implementation of an intervention, for example, observations provide data about how the intervention is delivered (the techniques) and how individuals respond to the intervention techniques. Observations also might be used to evaluate the use of target strategies in real-life contexts (i.e., generalization of outcomes). For example, children might be observed in a social setting to examine their use of target social skills. Approaches to observation may range from unstructured (ongoing participant observation) to highly structured (e.g., when process evaluators wish to observe and record specific instances of predesignated behaviors in a standardized period of time).

Logs/journals/narratives. Logs, journals, and narratives are techniques that involve the recording of data by program participants (e.g., facilitators, recipients), thus constituting a type of self-report. Logs provide a written record of activities; for example, facilitators keep a record of which intervention activities are implemented for the purpose of program documentation. Journals or narratives are the personal recordings of individuals' experiences and/or reactions to those experiences. To assess generalization, program recipients might be asked to keep journals, recording in a notebook their use of target skills in real-life settings. Alternatively, facilitators might be asked to keep narrative notes about their perceptions of the intervention process and the impact on recipients.

Cross Reference: See Book 2, Chapters 4 and 5, for more information on recording techniques

Curriculum-based assessment/artifacts. Curriculum-based assessment/artifacts are integral components or products of the intervention process. Curriculum-based assessment refers to curriculum exercises or activities that also yield research or evaluation data. For example, role-playing exercises can serve the dual purposes of providing practice in target skills and an opportunity for evaluators to observe the level of skill development. Artifacts are tangible products of the intervention and also constitute a potential source of data. For example, worksheets that participants complete as a part of an exercise can provide information about what they have learned.

Ethnographic surveys. Ethnographic surveys are self-report questionnaires (self-administered or administered through interviewing) developed on the basis of formative ethnographic data, such as a self-report measure of sexual practices that is based on data collected through in-depth interviews or focus groups (see also Trotter & Schensul, 1998, for a discussion of ethnographically informed surveys). Ethnographic surveys can be described as culture-specific instru-

Cross Reference: See Book 2, Chapter 8, on the construction of ethnographically informed surveys

ments because their content is specific to the culture of the target population. These surveys can be used in program planning, implementation, or evaluation.

Cross Reference: See Book 3, Chapter 3, for more information about elicitation techniques

Listings and pilesorts. Listings, pilesorts, and other elicitation techniques are used to gain an understanding of how participants conceptually organize or map a cultural domain (e.g., mother-daughter relationships). Individuals are asked to list items in a domain (e.g., "activities"). The items mentioned most often are used as the basis for pilesorting (e.g., activities mentioned might be: watch television, play football, clean house, go to the store, play hopscotch, go to dance classes). Participants are given a set of cards with the items and asked to sort them. Specific guidelines can be presented to guide sorting (e.g., sort in three piles, sort by gender, sort by age group). Consistency or consensus across respondents suggests culturally specific definitions.

USING ETHNOGRAPHY IN PROGRAM DEVELOPMENT: CASE STUDIES

In this section, we describe the use of ethnography to strengthen and evaluate intervention programs by using two community-based intervention projects, one conducted in North America and one in Southeast Asia, as case examples. We begin with a description of the two projects—the Urban Women Against Substance Abuse Program (UWASA), located in Hartford, Connecticut, and the Sexual Risk Prevention Project (SRPP), based in Sri Lanka. In each case example, ethnographic techniques were used specifically for the purposes of designing, monitoring, and evaluating culture-specific, theory-driven interventions. Both projects embodied a participatory model of program development. We describe how ethnography contributed to the participatory process by involving the stakeholders on a continual basis. Our case examples are organized by program phase. We describe the use of specific ethnographic techniques during specific phases of program development and explain why we made choices about which techniques we chose at that point in time. We also detail some of the information generated by these techniques and show how it directly contributed to program enhancement and evaluation.

Urban Women Against Substance Abuse

Case Study

Urban Women Against Substance Abuse (UWASA)[1] is a community-based research and demonstration intervention project for urban African American and Puerto Rican girls 9 to 12 years of age, as well as their female caregivers, who are living in low-income, high-risk neighborhoods in the city of Hartford, Connecticut. The purpose of the project is to build resilience to substance abuse and reduce the prevalence of drug use and other risky behaviors in adolescent girls. Specific program objectives include the following:

- Fostering the co-construction of preventive group norms with regard to avoidance of alcohol, tobacco, drugs, and risky sexual practices
- Improving risk recognition, communication, negotiation, critical thinking, and decision-making skills among girls
- Fostering cultural, ethnic, and gender identity as a means of enhancing self-esteem in girls
- Strengthening communication and understanding between mothers and daughters
- Evaluating program process and outcomes

The 9-month intervention consists of twice-weekly, 90-minute, after-school training sessions; sharing sessions among girls and their female caregivers following completion of each instructional module; supplemental cultural and recreational activities; and a community action research project. The program uses an ecological model, identifying risk and resilience factors at the individual, family, peer, neighborhood, school, community, and societal levels. Social construction and empowerment theories embedded in principles of action research drive the intervention model, which targets the development of resistance skills in girls; changes in their peer group; and changes in school, community, and societal policies and practices that increase exposure to behavioral risks.

Using predesignated group facilitation techniques, staff:

- Enable girls to identify cultural norms that either enhance or reduce risky behaviors or identify differences between the two
- Promote discussions of differences of opinion about these norms or negotiation of conflict
- Assist girls in identifying options for resistance
- Encourage the group to arrive at consensus with regard to the establishment of new group resistance norms

The facilitation skills used in the process are adapted from Nastasi and DeZolt (1994) and are as follows:

- Modeling (demonstrating target process or skill)
- Scaffolding (building on current skills to guide participants toward skill development in a step-by-step manner)
- Explication (articulating the problem-solving process)
- Reflection (identifying and evaluating target skill level)

Target outcomes include the following:

- An increase in positive attitudes against alcohol, tobacco, and other drug (ATOD) use
- Improved decision-making skills
- Improved positive peer intimacy and a corresponding decrease in peer pressure toward ATOD use
- Improvement in school attachment
- Increased knowledge about and resilience against HIV/AIDS and premature sexual activity

The program includes a component designed to appeal to mothers or "other mothers" (principal female caregivers who might be grandmothers, aunts, or even close friends of the mothers). This component includes weekly meetings, written correspondence, phone calls, and home visits. The purpose of these activities is to improve mother-daughter communication and relationships, which can serve as protective factors in high-risk urban environments. Action research (cf. Schensul & Schensul, 1978; Stringer, 1996), an empowerment strategy, frames the community project in which girls use their new skills to negotiate and carry out a project designed to increase their knowledge of a risk behavior area (e.g., runaway youth). The project produces materials that the girls use to build resiliency norms in their peers or to promote prevention policies in their schools, communities, and through the media.

Case Study

The Sexual Risk (HIV/AIDS) Prevention Project (SRPP)[2]

The SRPP was a community-based pilot intervention program for urban adolescents and young adults of both genders who were between the ages of 17 and 27 and resided in a low-income urban area of Kandy, a city in the central highlands of Sri Lanka (Nastasi, Schensul, et al., 1998-1999; Silva et al., 1997). The purpose of the project was prevention of sexual risk, specifically HIV/AIDS. Specific program objectives were the following:

- Improve communication and social negotiation in heterosexual relationships as antecedents to sexual-risk prevention behaviors
- Enable avoidance of sexual risk through recognition of the link between sexual behaviors and risky sexual practices
- Facilitate informed sexual risk decision making and negotiation with partners by increasing knowledge of reproductive health, sexually transmitted diseases (STDs), and HIV/AIDS
- Evaluate the use of dilemmas as a tool for improving conceptual understanding of sexual risk and social negotiation skills necessary to avoid risk by choosing safe sexual practices

The intervention process and content of the SRPP were based on extensive formative research conducted by a joint interdisciplinary team of Sri Lankan and North American researchers (anthropologists, sociologists, psychologists, and physicians) working with a local Sri Lankan field team. Using formative research findings, interventionists adapted for use with Sri Lankan youth a culturally responsive theory of group intervention developed in the United States. Critical features of the intervention were the following:

- The focus on sexual knowledge, attitudes, risk perception, decision making, and behavior
- Cultural specificity of content and language
- Peer facilitation
- Use of a social construction model of intervention (i.e., use of group process to foster cognitive and behavior change)
- Use of a collaborative consultation model for training of peer educators (i.e., interventionists and peer educators worked together throughout implementation to ensure that the program was conducted with integrity)

PROGRAM DESIGN/PLANNING

The purpose of ethnography during the initial phase of program development is to conduct formative research, gather insights from key informants, and identify needs and resources of the target population. The methods chosen should elicit exploratory data. In-depth or group interviews with people from the target community who are culturally knowledgeable help program designers understand intervention issues from the perspective of those who are directly affected. Because this phase often occurs prior to funding, the selected methods should be time- and cost-effective. Special attention must be paid to how to enter the field. For example, it is important to consider whether or not to gain access to issues and target populations through existing networks.

In preparation for intervention programming, information is gathered to develop a culture-specific theory of behavior change, frame the content and process of the intervention, and develop evaluation instruments.

Definition: Culture-specific interventions incorporate key cultural constructs as defined by members of the target population

Ethnography contributes to creating **culture-specific interventions**; that is, interventions that incorporate key cultural constructs as defined by members of the target population. The goal of cultural specificity is to foster acceptance of the intervention by the target population and increase the potential for institutionalization. Using a participatory model during this initial phase, program designers seek to initiate collaborative relationships with key stakeholders who become partners in data collection and program planning. Ethnography facilitates such linking of data collection and community organizing.

UWASA. In UWASA, ethnography was used at three critical junctures in the planning and development stage. Focus group discussions with youth and women, including mother-daughter pairs, were used to produce information that was transformed into the program model described in the grant proposal and the first draft of the curriculum. These data also helped to build a local constituency for the project. Institute for Community Research (ICR) program planners conducted a series of focus group interviews with African American and Puerto Rican women and youth associated with other programs of the ICR. Five meetings took place with African American and Puerto Rican women, during which discussion proceeded from the general (e.g., "What are the major issues facing adolescent girls in Hartford?") to more specific and sensitive topics, such as sexual risk, domestic and community violence, and perceptions of risks to which adolescent girls could be exposed. In-depth interviews were conducted with a subset of the women to gain better understanding of these topics from the women's perspective.

Prior program experience and existing theory and research led to the following important initial points of reference:

- Adolescents often have problems associated with family relationships and communication breakdowns.

- Many low-income urban women would like support in addressing their own concerns about how to manage the situations that their daughters encounter while growing up in high-risk environments.
- Information is limited with respect to how African American and Latina girls experience adolescence, and the role of mothers in the girls' maturation process.

The women were asked to speculate on risk and protective factors relevant to adolescent girls in their community. They identified and described the following risk factors: gang recruitment; lack of cultural identity; widespread exposure to ATOD; sale of alcohol and tobacco to minors; sexual and physical abuse in families; high rates of crime; HIV infection; injection drug use; prostitution; violence; lack of after-school programs for adolescent girls, especially for those who were living on their own; and lack of positive friendship groupings. They also identified and described several protective factors, including closely knit three- to five-generation families; desire to leave Aid to Families with Dependent Children; spirituality; and local resources that promoted ethnic, racial, and cultural identity and intercultural bonding.

Convinced that working with girls alone would not address issues between the young women and their caregivers, the women suggested a parallel mother-daughter program for girls ages 9 to 12. They felt that a joint program would empower both the women and the girls by offering them, separately and together, training, cultural and political history, spiritual and emotional development, counseling, case management, and alternative activities. Their view was that separate sessions would foster personal growth and an improved self-concept, while facilitated joint sessions would provide a forum to discuss and resolve sensitive issues. The women also identified the range of family structures in the community and urged that the definition of "mother" be expanded to include grandmothers and "other mothers"/*tias* (terms used to extend the family in Black and Puerto Rican contexts in the Northeast). They suggested that this approach would expand support for girls, minimize intergenerational conflict, and foster attention to sensitive issues such as intergenerational abuse.

Data also were gathered from youth through informal discussions, in-depth interviews, and a series of focus group discussions conducted at a formal retreat with young people from another ICR youth action research program. Youth identified many of the same concerns—widespread availability and use of drugs and alcohol, daily exposure to violence, and few after-school activities. Teens also identified new risk factors, such as the following:

- The reluctance to talk with mothers about drugs and sex
- Physical abuse
- The appeal of gang membership and selling drugs
- Holding drug money for boyfriends
- The lack of intellectual challenge at school
- Presence of drug dealers outside their schools and in their families
- The use of marijuana in school bathrooms
- The lack of money for college
- The absence of career counseling in school

The teens identified as protective factors the love of family members, availability of female nonkin, learning about their own ethnic identity and gaining personal and cultural pride, doing joint projects on social issues that require "taking things apart" (analysis), finishing school, making money through a job, teaching leadership skills to other teens, and reducing interethnic fear by engaging in activities with young people of different ethnic groups.

Youth stressed the importance of creating projects and curricula through which they could learn about their own ethnic and cultural history. They reasoned that these activities helped prevent ATOD use and other risk involvement because young people gained a sense of personal pride and community affiliation.

Key point

Focus group participants also were asked to help develop the problem statement that would guide the intervention research program. Questions were used to stimulate group discussion and debate about risk factors, or factors that relate to, cause, or precede the problem. Using circle and line diagrams, women and teens described how factors were related. The groups constructed their understanding of these relationships and came to general agreement about the interaction among factors. Through these techniques, stakeholders were able to build a theoretical model. In the process, they had decided on a central problem (i.e., reducing risky behavior and building resilience). Addressing this issue became the project goal. The primary factors identified as contributing to it became the specific objectives targeted for intervention.

Key informants also specified many critical programmatic elements that were included in the intervention design. For example, both teens and women endorsed the provision of separate but parallel curricula for women and girls, but teens were emphatic about the need for well-articulated rules regarding how and whether program staff would share with the mothers information revealed by the girls could be shared by program staff with mothers.

These ethnographic data produced a project design that combined elements supported by theory and research and by the cultural experiences and perspectives of the target population. The culture-specific UWASA conceptual model that resulted from this process is presented in Table 1.2.

Once funded, ethnographic techniques—including focus groups with women associated with the communities in which the program was to be conducted, participant observation in programs serving girls of the target age group, and interviews with women and girls—enabled the

TABLE 1.2 UWASA Conceptual Model

	Outcomes	
Intervention–Training Focus	*Intermediate Outcomes*	*Final Outcomes*
Positive peer clusters Ethnic and gender identity Awareness of adolescent development Preventive alcohol, tobacco, and drug knowledge, attitudes, behaviors, and norms Research action and inquiry skill development Decision-making and conflict resolution skills	Improved daughter/mother communication Improved mother/daughter intimacy Improved girls' self-concept Improved peer intimacy and positive social influence	Improved anti-ATOD protective knowledge and attitudes Improvement in reported risk behaviors Improved school attachment

investigators and new staff to fine tune and strengthen the intervention. The result was elimination of one target group, adaptation of the program plans to align with mothers' identified needs and perspectives, and sharpening of the curriculum to make it more responsive to topics raised and to the developmental stages represented by the girls in the program.

Next a series of focus groups (6 to 10 members per group) was conducted with girls (representing daughters) and women (representing mothers) from each of the three target neighborhoods. Sometimes, mother-daughter pairs participated; at other times, only girls or only women joined the discussion groups. Focus group members were asked to comment on the following topics:

- Program format and curriculum
- Assessment instruments
- Issues of importance to girls/women
- Target areas for personal growth
- Cultural or development issues that were likely to constitute sensitive topics

- Concerns about mother-daughter interactions during the intervention
- Their views on community action projects

The focus groups with women yielded the following findings:

- Women wished to address their own needs as well as the needs of their daughters.
- Mothers were concerned about their daughters' conflicts over ethnic identity and peer pressure regarding school achievement (i.e., pressure to underachieve).
- The women were concerned about whether their daughters wanted to and could meet the mothers' expectations for them.
- Mothers recognized that their own lives might provide negative models for their daughters, and they expressed discomfort about openly sharing their feelings and life concerns with their daughters.
- Women expressed concern about their ability to participate in an action research project, given their responsibilities.

Findings from the girls' focus groups illustrated the challenges they faced daily at home, at school, and with their friends. Girls were conflicted over their ethnic, cultural, and racial identity. Although some of them wished to cross ethnic and cultural boundaries, they found it difficult in environments that reinforced social segregation. Dark-skinned Puerto Ricans, light-skinned African Americans, and girls of mixed backgrounds expressed special problems with being forced to choose and align themselves with one group or another. Girls were adamant about not wanting to share with their mothers any information about their involvement with young men. Data from the focus groups signaled potential areas of conflict, suggested the need for resource and referral systems, and helped identify areas of misunderstanding or misinterpretation of assessment instruments.

SRPP. In the Sri Lankan sexual risk project, several ethnographic methods were used to conduct formative research and needs assessment (Silva et al., 1997). These included key informant interviews, in-depth interviews, participant observation, pilesorts, and ethnographic surveys. The purpose of ethnographic data collection was to gather information about personal and sociocultural factors related to sexual risk among youth and young adults. Specifically, data collection focused on gathering data about sexual knowledge, attitudes, and practices; sources of information about sexuality; potential for risk and perceptions of risk; protective strategies; available resources for seeking advice and help with sexual concerns; and the role of family, peer groups, and community in promoting safe sexual practices.

Preliminary data were collected through key informant interviews and participant observation. Key informant interviews were conducted with individuals who were particularly knowledgeable about sexual risk among youth and young adults. Key informants included health service providers, informal and formal leaders, and young adults from the target community. Observations were conducted in public settings frequented by young adults, including parks, "lovers' lanes," soccer fields, and bus stops.

Cross Reference: See Book 2, Chapter 5, for more information on conducting participant observation

Open-ended, structured (in-depth) individual interviews and ethnographic surveys (in-depth, self-report questionnaires) were used to gather more comprehensive information about relevant individual and sociocultural factors. Structured interviews were conducted with 156 male and female youth from a university campus ($n = 93$) and local community ($n = 63$). In addition, listings and pilesorts were conducted with a sample of young adults to provide additional information regarding the organization and sequencing of sexual practices.

Cross Reference: See Book 3, Chapter 3, for methods for listing and pilesorting

Data from the interviews and pilesorts were used to develop the content of the ethnographic survey, which was administered to 615 young adults—311 from the university

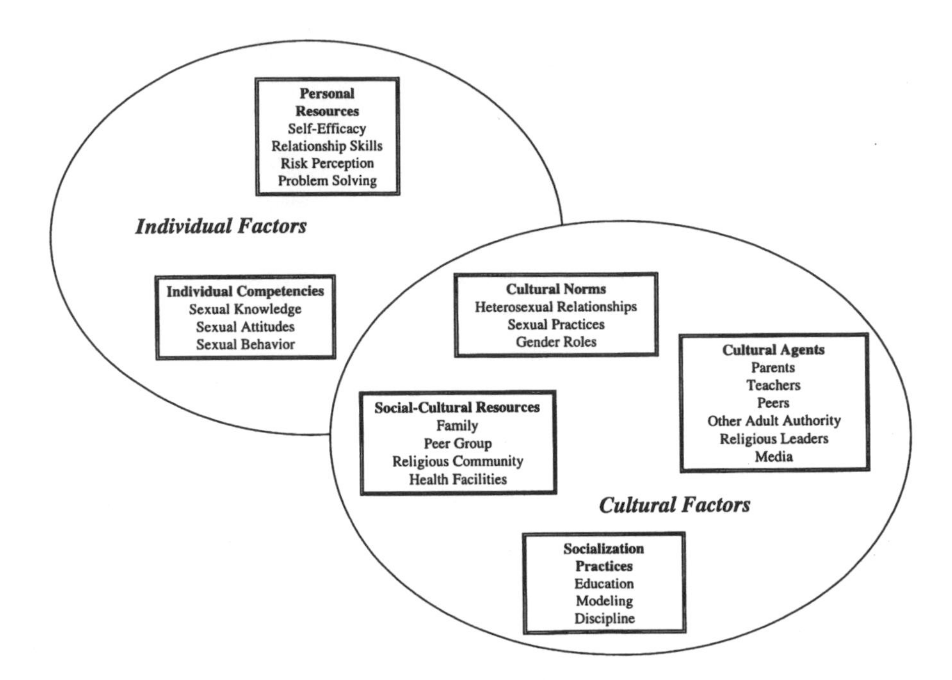

Figure 1.1. Model of sexual risk decision making. SOURCE: Reproduced from Nastasi, Schensul, et al., 1998-1999.

and 304 from the community. Eighty percent of the target community population (unmarried women and men ages 17 to 27) completed surveys which provided a comprehensive initial database regarding the individual and cultural factors outlined previously. The conceptual model resulting from this formative research is presented in Figure 1.1.

As in UWASA, the formative research data also influenced the design of the intervention in several ways (Nastasi, Schensul, et al., 1998-1999). First, information about sexual knowledge, attitudes, practices, and experiences of the population influenced the program curriculum. For example, real-life experiences of the target population provided the content for stories containing hypothetical dilemmas used to promote discussion and decision making about risky situations. Second, the role of peers as cultural agents who influenced sexual attitudes, norms, and practices became apparent and prompted the use of a peer facilitation model. Third, gender roles and gender differences influenced program design. For example, the power differences in heterosexual relationships as well as women's limited peer networks and vocabulary for discussing sex suggested the need to provide women with opportunities to develop and use their "voices," expand their knowledge of reproductive health and sexuality, and expand the female peer network. Fourth, cultural taboos on discussing sexuality prompted the use of a scaffolding technique in which participants were guided through a series of activities to develop knowledge, language, and a context for discussing sexuality. For example, we focused on general and friendship relationships before turning to romantic and sexual relationships. Initially, we used a numbered list of sex behaviors so that participants could discuss sexual practices by numbers without having to name them, which would have embarrassed the participants. Later on, they were able to refer to these terms by name. We also conducted discussions in same-gender groups before forming mixed-gender groups.

In a manner similar to that used in the UWASA project, ***SRPP program developers tailored existing intervention approaches to the specific culture of the target population.*** Program developers adopted social construction theory as the basis for designing the intervention. According to this theory, interpersonal exchange of ideas is essential to the transmission of culture as well as to the development of individual attitudes, thoughts, and behavior (Guisinger & Blatt, 1994; Nastasi & DeZolt, 1994; Rogoff, 1990; Vygotsky, 1978; Wertsch, 1991). Research supports the social construction process as a mechanism for fostering both cognitive (e.g., higher-order thinking, problem solving, learning) and personal-social growth (e.g., self-esteem, self-efficacy, interpersonal skills; Nastasi & Clements, 1991; Nastasi & DeZolt, 1994). A social construction model of sexual risk prevention integrates cultural (i.e., cultural norms, beliefs, values, socialization processes, and sociocultural resources)

Key point

and individual (i.e., knowledge, attitudes, practices, self-efficacy, risk perception, and relationship and problem-solving skills) factors, with the goal of influencing peer norms and individual competencies. The integration of culture-specific data and existing theory resulted in an intervention characterized by the following:

- The program used existing culture-specific norms and core values about relationships and sexuality that were identified in the formative research phase.
- Program participants engaged in a negotiated interpretation of the norms through their interactions with each other and with peer educators, public health workers, and professionals.
- Participants worked in small groups to gain accurate knowledge, examine existing norms, and discuss the role of norms in influencing decision making and risk behavior.
- Participants examined their perceptions of sexual and related risks.
- Participants practiced communication and decision making.

In the SRPP project, the group process was guided by peer educators, with support from public health professionals and paraprofessionals.

Furthermore, by employing a participatory model, SRPP researcher and program development teams were able to involve community members in formative research and the program design process. For example, young adults from the target population assisted in conducting structured interviews, pilesorts, and ethnographic surveys. In addition, the peer educators, selected from the community, participated in program design. Public health professionals and paraprofessionals from the target culture were involved in decision making about data collection, data interpretation, and program design. This involvement was especially significant because of the socially sensitive nature of the topic and program planners' concern that parents or community religious leaders might try to prevent the program from being carried out.

PROGRAM IMPLEMENTATION: DOCUMENTING PROCESS AND PROGRAM MODIFICATION

During program implementation, interventionist researchers collect ethnographic data to document and monitor the implementation process in order to ensure program integrity, make appropriate modifications to the program, and identify staff training needs. Data collection is conducted to address questions such as the following:

- Are program activities and techniques being carried out according to the program design (i.e., is the program being implemented with integrity)?
- Are participants progressing toward stated goals and objectives? If not, what changes need to be made in the program? Is additional staff training needed?

Ethnographic data collection during implementation helps to keep the program on course and ensure that essential components are being implemented. It is also used to document what actually occurs and why. In this section, we describe how ***ethnography fosters reflective practice by interventionists and facilitators and enables program evaluators to give immediate and responsive feedback.*** The use of ethnography to monitor progress toward program goals is addressed in the later section on program evaluation.

Key point

UWASA

Ethnographic methods used during implementation of the UWASA project included direct observation, logs/journals and narratives maintained by staff and participants, pilesorts, and curriculum-based assessment and artifacts, some of which are included in participant portfolios. *Direct observation* techniques were used to document program integrity and provide feedback to program staff. Observers focused on facilitators' use of intervention techniques, and whether and how planned activities were carried out; participants' responses to facilitator techniques; and participants' interactions with each other during group activities (see Appendix A).

Evaluators observed a representative sample of sessions. A trained observer attended each of these sessions and produced ethnographic fieldnotes describing the session as well as a detailed narrative description of the facilitator's use of intervention techniques. In addition, a subsample of the observed sessions were videotaped in order to document group process (i.e., the ways in which the participants interacted with each other, the facilitators, and other adults in the room). The videocamera emphasized participants' body language and conversation. The verbal and nonverbal behaviors of a preselected social unit (a pair of girls, a small or large group) were recorded during an entire curriculum activity so that interactions could be followed from the beginning of the activity to the end and linked with facilitator behaviors. The videotapes supplement the direct observation notes and provide a tool for assessing the reliability of observational data recorded by evaluators. They also serve as a tool for staff development.

Cross Reference: See Book 3, Chapter 1, on use of audiovisual data recoding methods

With regard to using videotapes for staff development, facilitators are able to view tapes of themselves in private or with training consultants in order to evaluate the ways in which they are using facilitation techniques, as well as to determine their additional training needs. This process can facilitate **reflective practice or self-evaluation**—a process in which facilitators make explicit, self-observe, and evaluate their own use of the program's intervention strategies. In addition, observational data document variation in implementation techniques and group responses across facilitators, sessions, and participants. They can be used to identify

Definition: Reflective practice or self-evaluation is a process in which facilitators make explicit, observe, and evaluate their use of the program's intervention strategies

and distinguish essential components of the intervention (i.e., those believed to be related to program outcomes) from other components that may be interesting but unrelated to program outcomes, or innovative and useful, and subsequently incorporated into the program's implementation protocols. Finally, videotaped segments can be used for dissemination and replication of the program.

In the UWASA project, *facilitator logs and narratives* are used for two purposes: to help program staff engage in reflective practice and to provide program documentation and monitoring. At the completion of each session, the facilitator completes the session log or checklist, indicating whether and to what degree program objectives are met, whether planned activities are carried out, and whether the facilitator views the session as successful. In addition, facilitators provide explanations when activities are not carried out as intended or when activities are considered unsuccessful. They are encouraged to record any other impressions of the session in the log, using a narrative recording format (see Appendix B). These logs provide a record of session activities and an opportunity for program staff both to reflect on sessions and their performance and to identify areas of need (i.e., for program modification or staff training).

Key point 

Content analysis of facilitator logs helps interventionists and evaluators examine critical dimensions of the program. For example, logs provide information in the UWASA project about the extent to which target concepts (e.g., ethnic identity formation) are addressed across the curriculum, and how the facilitator's understanding and application of intervention techniques has changed over the course of the year or over the entire period of the intervention.

Curriculum-based assessment is used extensively in the UWASA project to gather data that allow immediate adaptation of curricular activities to address the needs of the participants without varying the core content or session objectives. Curricular activities are designed to provide knowledge and to shape attitudes and behaviors relevant to the session topic. These activities are particularly helpful for producing new information and artifacts related to specific issues (e.g., HIV/AIDS, violence, and the formation of gender identity) and for documenting individual and group progress. For example, at the beginning of a unit on violence, curricular activities provided the basis for examination of girls' understanding of violence. The girls first brainstormed a list of behaviors that they considered to be violent. They listed extreme acts such as rape and murder as "violent" and, in response to probes, said that they considered behaviors such as yelling or name calling to be "not violent." The women, when presented with the same exercise, identified psychological problems, such as depression, as violent.

For each of the items identified, participants made a label. These labels were used in a pilesort activity. In separate groups, the girls and women negotiated the placement of the items. First, individuals—girls and women separately—placed each act identified as violent on a grid using a 3-point Likert scale, with "degree of violence" on the horizontal axis (e.g., fist fighting is "not violent," "a little violent," or "very violent") and "level of acceptability" of the behavior on the vertical axis (e.g., fist fighting is "never OK," "sometimes OK," or "always OK"). Next, the girls and women, working in separate groups, negotiated the placement of the items on the same grid, arriving at consensus on each item.

Over the course of the project, intervention activities and research on the role of violence in the girls' lives continued. For example, an exercise was designed to assess how girls perceive their ability to avoid, resist, or cope with violent situations. Bags of sand symbolically representing different forms of violence were packed into a suitcase that each girl had to carry. The activity involved groups of six to eight girls in a discussion of the types of violence they would like to remove from their suitcase (and, by analogy, from their lives), and which individual-, peer-, family-, or other-adult-supported strategies they might use to accomplish this. Following the group activity, each girl took a shopping bag and filled it with sandbags representing violence in her own life. She then reflected in her journal on the personal impact of each type of violence, how it occurs, how she might vary her actions/reactions to it, ways to avoid certain risk-provoking environments or situations, and the possibility of developing more positive coping mechanisms.

Staff then use information from the exercises, in conjunction with the facilitation technique known as scaffolding, to encourage girls both individually and as a group to consider and develop strategies that could reduce or minimize the negative effects of violence on their lives. Participants' responses are documented by the evaluation team (and sometimes by program staff) as part of the project assessment. This becomes especially important when exercises are deepened or repeated, and documentation allows the program staff to see how group and individual responses change over time, in line with program goals and objectives. The results of exercises are often kept for reference and as "artifacts." These materials are used for planning subsequent sessions, for example, in this instance, to further explore participants' definitions and perceptions of violence and their responses to acts of violence. Some exercises are systematically repeated at the end of the unit as an outcome evaluation strategy in order to assess changes in individual and group responses to the intervention.

Another set of learning activities was used to explore the process of gender identity formation. The following examples demonstrate how art and drawing were used to help 9- to 12-year-old girls think about and discuss complex constructs such as gender and kinship. One exercise was designed to investigate the girls' perceptions of gender roles and expectations. It was organized as part of a session that included learning stations with activities focused on gender, ethnic, and cultural identity. At one station, girls were given slips of paper listing a range of activities and asked to paste activities that "girls do" or "boys do" on two overlapping paper dolls, one representing a male and the other a female, with the overlapping area meant to include activities shared by both. Girls were organized into pairs. They were then asked to discuss the following questions using their own individual interpretations:

- Which roles are performed only by girls, only by boys, or both?
- Which activities do girls and boys continue to do when they become women or men? What do they stop doing? What accounts for the changes?
- How do the roles and actions of girls/women in your homes compare to roles of girls/women you admire?
- How can you talk about and negotiate different roles for yourselves within your households if you wish to?

In addition to *curriculum-embedded data collection* techniques, a sample of 11 girls was interviewed between one and four times. The interviewer, a graduate anthropology student,[3] used art-based exercises to give girls alternative ways of expressing and explaining their ideas. For example, to help the girls describe and discuss complex family relationships, the intern gave them colored shapes and symbols to construct a kinship chart. Kinship denotes culturally defined relationships among individuals who share family ties. The girls were provided with the following symbols:

- Circle = females
- Triangle = males
- Square = self/ego
- Lines show marriage, sibling ties, and descent; cross-hatch lines show divorce and separation
- X = death

The girls associated each symbol that they used with specific initials. They pasted the symbols and lines on construction paper showing three generations of people to whom they were related or considered family. They located individuals who currently lived in their household within a house-shaped frame and those who resided elsewhere outside of the frame. The interviewer helped the girls construct the chart, using this as an opportunity to discuss household demographics and roles.

Weekly debriefing sessions provide the opportunity for program and evaluation staff to process material from observations, curriculum activities, narratives, and logs on a regular basis; identify areas requiring program adjustments or revisions; and signal the need for further staff training. Through systematic application of ethnographic data collection methods, we were able to provide feedback that could be used immediately for program improvement. For example, observations of sessions indicated that when girls misbehaved or acted out, it was impossible to implement the instructional procedures that were critical to testing the theory of prevention used in the program. Discussions between evaluation and program staff resulted in the recognition that staff needed additional training in behavior management. We were able to institute staff training and curriculum adaptations to address these concerns.

We also used curriculum-based data collection to increase our understanding of the meaning of violence and the anger that UWASA girls and women so frequently expressed. Observation of sessions, review of materials, and informal interviews with girls revealed that verbally and physically abusive behavior is often the norm among peers, between parents and children, and among siblings. Anger and violent behavior are manifested in girls' involvement in gang activity (as revealed in their artwork and discussions recorded in small-group work); verbal and physical outbursts in the sessions; and girls' inclusion of violent language and acts of violence in their discussions and in the development of stories, role-plays, and "dilemmas." Evaluation and program staff and a staff social worker used written and videotaped observations to identify the sequencing of events that led to outbursts of anger and the factors that triggered specific types of expressions of anger. In addition, program staff members could use the observational data to identify the most effective activities and facilitator techniques for addressing these behaviors in training sessions and for helping the group to develop alternatives to angry outbursts that could be generalized to their life situations.

SRPP

Ethnographic methods used during implementation of the sexual risk project included the use of logs by facilitators and participants, participant observation, and curriculum-based assessment. These assessment techniques were integrated into the routine of the intervention process and provided valuable data about how the program was being implemented, the need for program modification and staff training, the response of participants to program activities, and the extent to which program activities were having the intended impact. The latter was relevant to both program modification and evaluation of effectiveness.

Key point

In addition to using formative research to identify individual and sociocultural factors within the target population, ***we also sought to ensure cultural specificity of the intervention through a recursive process linking assessment and intervention.*** That is, data collected during each session were used to modify intervention content and activities to address the needs of program participants.

Activity and facilitator logs were completed by peer educators after every session. The activity log, in checklist format, included a list of planned session activities; facilitators were asked to indicate which activities were completed and the success of each activity, and to provide additional comments about the session (i.e., their own reflections on the process and on their own performance). Peer educators also completed a facilitator log (checklist) on which they indicated which instructional strategies were used during the session. Participants completed a similar *participant log* (self-evaluation of group process) on which they indicated the nature of their participation and the quality of group process. This form was completed as a group and thus involved discussion of group participation and process and consensus building. (Copies of these logs are presented in Appendix C.) The data generated from these logs were used to document the intervention process. They also served a self-evaluative function; that is, both facilitators and participants came to use these forms as a self-check of their participation.

Participant observation was conducted by the intervention support staff (professionals) and by the group members. The support staff was present for all sessions to provide on-site consultation to peer educators and to monitor program implementation. The staff conducted informal observations of program activities and responded to queries from peer educators when difficulties arose. These informal observations and interactions with peer educators provided important information about the need for program modification and/or staff training. This information was used to guide weekly feedback and ongoing training sessions. A group member (participant) was designated to record the discussion that occurred during each session. Recorders were instructed to document both individual comments and group consensus, and to review their notes for accuracy with group members at the end of each session. In addition, peer educators reviewed notes for accuracy following each session. These observation notes provided a critical database for examining the nature of group process and the evolution of participants' knowledge, attitudes, concepts, and target skills. For example, the observation notes provided data about the processes of discussion and consensus building among group members, both of which were critical elements of the intervention.

Curriculum-based assessment activities also provided a database of artifacts for examining changes related to program objectives. In addition to the written record of discussions, participants also completed individual and group worksheets for each session. The combination of worksheets and session notes provided data about culture-specific norms, practices, and concepts of individuals as well as those shared by the participants. These data supplemented formative research data collected previously. For example, worksheets and session notes from an activity focused on defining "sexual risk" provided additional information about participants' definitions of sexual behavior and perceptions of sexual risk that extended our existing understanding of these constructs in the Sri Lankan youth culture.

PROGRAM EVALUATION

Program evaluators can use ethnographic data collection methods to evaluate program acceptability (e.g., staff and participant perceptions of program feasibility), integrity (whether key elements of the program are implemented appropriately), and effectiveness (existence of changes in the direction of program goals and presence of positive or negative outcomes). Continuous data collection focused on outcomes can simultaneously facilitate ongoing monitoring of progress and enhance our understanding of the process of knowledge, cognitive, attitudinal, and behavior change. In addition, documentation of the implementation process provides evidence of program integrity and makes possible the examination of the links between process (i.e., program elements), immediate impact, and longer term outcomes. Ethnographic evaluation data on outcomes can be used to sup- plement quantitative measures, thus facilitating multi- method assessment and methodological triangulation (Lincoln & Guba, 1985). Ethnographic methods relevant to evaluation include the full range of techniques outlined in an earlier section. We now examine the use of particular techniques within the context of the UWASA and SRPP projects.

Cross Reference: See Books 1, 2, and 5 for methods used in program evaluation

UWASA

Ethnography is used for evaluation purposes in the UWASA project to develop and adapt instruments that measure predicted outcomes of the intervention, assess individual and group development, and evaluate and interpret outcomes. Methods include the following:

- Participant and direct observation of intervention and testing sessions
- Review of materials produced by the girls
- Periodic, in-depth interviewing
- Informal interviewing of participants during sessions breaks, at snack time, during downtime, or during field trips

Key point 

Ethnography was used to inform the modification of local outcome instruments to ensure that they had meaning for the target population and were directly related to the intervention. The adaptation of an HIV/AIDS pre-post test instrument, which was developed in line with initial curricula, illustrates this process. After observing sessions and interviewing girls on their understanding of sexuality and HIV transmission, an existing HIV/AIDS evaluation instrument was improved by removing items judged to be developmentally inappropriate. The modified instrument was administered to girls in UWASA and to two matched comparison groups, and the outcomes were evaluated. Items were tested for reliability, and revised HIV/AIDS knowledge and intention scales were constructed. The scales were then integrated into the overall study's battery of pre- and posttest instruments.

Curriculum-based techniques that build research methods into specific exercises allow interventionists and evaluators to use materials that are generated, along with observations and guided interviewing, to assess individual and group development over time. For example, UWASA seeks to improve decision-making skills. One component in the instructional process encourages participants to generate a range of possible alternative courses of action with respect to addressing dilemmas or social problems they may encounter, and to consider consequences relative to each course of action. To master this skill, girls must first be able to increase the number of realistic options that they can generate. Reviewing materials produced by individual girls and groups and using guided interviewing, evaluators are able to assess how both individual participants, as well as the intervention group, are progressing along this dimension.

Observation also provides the opportunity for interventionists and evaluators to assess the degree to which target skills are incorporated into the repertoires of each participant. Observation of sessions generates information relative to acquisition of a target skill (e.g., negotiating different perspectives) through planned activities (e.g., role playing or solving a dilemma without explicit instructions). Observation of unstructured activities, such as snack time, permits evaluators and interventionists to gather data about whether and how the target skill is being generalized to real-life situations. Periodic systematic observation of the intervention is critical to determining whether the intervention is actually being delivered as planned. Another important role for observation occurs when formal outcome measures are being administered. The degree to which research participants understand what they are to do when taking the test or answering interviewer questions, conditions under which the test is administered, receptivity of participants to written test-taking, how tired they act—all influence the quality of the data being collected. Observation of testing sessions is a very useful—though little discussed—procedure that can help to interpret outcome results.

Finally, continuous formal and informal *ethnographic interviewing* of facilitators and participants is used throughout a project to help assess and understand all aspects of the intervention and its outcomes. Interviews are used in conjunction with other methods to illuminate the meanings associated with materials or activities from the perspective of staff, women, and youth. In this manner, the acceptability of the intervention, as well as its integrity and effectiveness, can be assessed.

SRPP

Evaluation of the SRPP program included the use of several ethnographic techniques, including participant observation, informal interviews, curriculum-based artifacts, and ethnographic surveys. Foci for evaluation were the following:

- Program acceptability (i.e., peer educators' and participants' satisfaction with program activities and content, as well as perceptions of program effectiveness)
- Program integrity (i.e., documentation of the implementation of program content and activities, with careful attention to consistency across groups)
- Program effectiveness (outcomes)

Measures of acceptability included a self-report *ethnographic questionnaire/survey* designed specifically for the project and culture, and *group discussion* of open-ended evaluation questions. These measures were administered during the final intervention session. The questionnaires were designed by interventionists to assess participants' and peer educators' perceptions of the program's effectiveness for providing knowledge and guiding future behavior related to relationships, reproductive health, STDs and HIV/AIDS, prevention of STDs and HIV/AIDS, and decision making. The open-ended questions addressed positive and negative features of the program, perceived benefits of the program, motivation for participation, and suggestions for change. Open-ended questions were discussed as a group, and a designated recorder within each group recorded participants' responses. Responses to questionnaires and written documentation of the discussion constituted the database for program acceptability. In addition, ongoing interactions (informal interviews) and participant observation during the intervention sessions and weekly training sessions provided information about acceptability on a continual basis.

The ongoing nature of this data collection facilitated the strengthening of the program through program modifications and additional staff training. The data collected at the termination of the project provided information about ways to enhance both programming and staff training in the future. For example, participants requested additional sessions on relationship and decision-making skills, as well as more opportunities to engage in mixed-gender discussions. At a follow-up session, peer educators expressed interest in learning how to communicate the content of the curriculum to peers within informal community contexts.

Integrity measures included the peer educator and participant logs, participant observation, and curriculum-based artifacts described in the implementation section. The logs provided documentation of satisfactory completion of all program activities and adherence to facilitator behaviors and group process.

Narrative notes of peer educators (on logs), session observation notes, and artifacts provided detailed information about variability of program implementation (e.g., in peer educator skill for disseminating information, answering questions, and facilitating group process). On-site consultation and weekly peer educator consultation/training sessions provided mechanisms for addressing implementation difficulties during the course of the session or program, respectively. For example, peer educators indicated concerns about the adequacy of their knowledge base in reproductive health and sexually transmitted diseases, particularly given the questions posed by participants. To address this issue, we solicited the help of public health educators, who attended subsequent sessions to answer participant questions.

Outcome (effectiveness) measures included an individually administered *ethnographic survey* (with content developed from the formative research database to reflect culture-specific language, experiences, and concepts) administered in the first and final program sessions. This survey measured sexual knowledge, attitudes, risk perception, and decision-making skills. The decision-making measure presented a scenario (dilemma) and open-ended questions designed to examine perception of risk, protection against risk, proposed actions, and confidence in performing proposed actions (see Appendix D).

The decision-making measure was particularly appropriate for evaluating program-specific outcomes. For example, open-ended responses to the problem-solving scenario reflected changes in risk perception and risk protection/prevention that were consistent with the content of the curriculum. In addition, postintervention similarities among the responses of members of respective small groups suggested that ideas expressed by individual group members prior to intervention were assimilated into the thinking of other group members. This finding provided evidence for the potential impact of group process in fostering consensus building and construction of shared norms regarding sexual risk prevention, and thus for the role of socially constructing such norms as a tool for intervention.

Furthermore, session notes and artifacts provided important information regarding the utility of the social construction process (the core of the intervention process) for facilitating cognitive change and skill development. For example, ***discussions during mixed-gender sessions provided evidence of the effectiveness of the social construction (discussion and consensus building) process for extending the repertoire of potential responses to sexual risk.*** For example, in one session, the young men and women acknowledged the differing perspectives of the boyfriend and girlfriend depicted in a hypothetical scenario, and they agreed that the two characters should "come to a settlement through a dialogue." In addition, the final solution reached by the group reflected integration of alternative ideas proposed by male and female group members.

Key point

THE UNIQUE CONTRIBUTIONS OF ETHNOGRAPHY TO PROGRAM DEVELOPMENT

Ethnography is both necessary and appropriate to achieving the purposes of each phase of program development as outlined in the preceding section. Using ethnographic methods can contribute to the process of program development. Ethnography can be used to involve participants and other stakeholders in providing input into program design, thus promoting greater acceptability and ownership of the intervention. For example, in developing a school-based mental health program, program developers can use focus groups with teachers to gather information about adjustment problems that they observe among students. Focus groups can serve to identify stakeholders' perceptions of needs and can involve teachers in formulating program objectives and identifying potential interventions that can be conducted in the classroom. In this way, stakeholders can be involved as partners in early decision making about program directions and content.

In *program planning*, ethnography helps to design programs that take the context of the situation and the culture of the participants into consideration. Ethnography moves program planners to take into consideration the perspectives or points of view of the target population. Another way to say this is that ethnography is a necessary tool for identifying the individual, contextual, and cultural variables that influence both the target problem and the solutions.

Using ethnography to study the cultural context of the target population can provide information that leads to adaptation of existing theory and intervention techniques. This permits program planners to tailor the intervention to the specific population, community, or context. For example, formative research using ethnographic methods conducted in a community in Sri Lanka (Silva et al., 1997) led to the development of a conceptual model of sexual risk decision making (depicted in Figure 1.1; Nastasi, Schensul, et al., 1998-1999) for understanding sexual risk and guiding the development of a risk prevention program.

Using ethnography, we are able to understand and identify critical norms, values, and beliefs that may influence the knowledge, attitudes, and behaviors of participants in relation to the desired changes. In addition, the study of culture, through ethnography, can provide insights into the socialization practices that influence the target phenomena and thus suggest appropriate intervention processes. ***A thorough understanding of the target culture, including its cultural norms, cultural agents, sociocultural resources, and***

Key point

socialization practices, is critical to developing culture-specific interventions and, ultimately, effecting sustainable changes.

Finally, the formative research conducted prior to or during program planning is useful for developing or modifying assessment tools that are specific to the population and culture. The formative research conducted in Sri Lanka guided the development of a baseline survey instrument to assess key individual (e.g., sexual knowledge, attitudes, practices) and sociocultural (e.g., family relationships, influence of peers on sexual knowledge and practices) variables. For example, the measure of sexual behavior in Sri Lanka was designed to reflect actual sexual practices in terms of the nature and sequence of interactions that characterized intimacy and sexual behaviors there (Silva et al., 1997).

During the *implementation phase,* ethnography has several uses. For example, as suggested in the case studies, observations and interviews can be used to:

- Document the integrity of intervention
- Identify the need to modify intervention content and/or process
- Identify the need for staff training
- Relate process to outcome

Videotaped observations can be used to:

- Examine interactions between facilitators and participants in groups
- Assess the relationships between those interactions and program outcomes
- Provide examples of effective interactions

Ethnography is critical to describing and monitoring the process of change. It is also an approach that is useful in studying natural phenomena. Thus, it can provide the methodology for describing the evolution of the intervention process and its effect on individual and environmental factors. Using ethnography involves an iterative or recursive process of continuous data collection, analysis, and reflection that results in changes in intervention. In this way, programmers can strengthen or extend interventions in a continuous manner, thus ensuring close links between assessment and intervention. For example, examination of the content of discussions during an initial pilot of a sexual risk prevention program with peer educators in Sri Lanka indicated that "virginity" was a recurring theme in discussions across many topics (e.g., relationships, sexuality, communication) and convinced program developers of the need to focus specific sessions on the topic of virginity and to address loss of virginity as a culturally specific sexual risk (Nastasi, Schensul, et al., 1998-1999). Similar data collected in UWASA sessions on violence and anger were incorporated into facilitator training and the program curriculum.

In *program evaluation,* ethnography ensures that evaluators capture the views of program participants about their experience of the program, the program's acceptability, and whether or not the program has had an influence on their thinking or behavior (or both). In addition, ethnographic documentation of the intervention process helps to ensure understanding of the role that individual, cultural, and contextual factors play in effecting or inhibiting change. Furthermore, the detailed description that results from thorough ethnographic study is critical to future replication or transferability of successful programs. Thus, documentation of the intervention methods and content can be used to produce program manuals that provide not only program content and interventions and techniques, but also a description of possible modifications in response to difficulties that facilitators might encounter. For example, the alternative techniques for discussing sexual interactions that are developed in response to participant reluctance to talk about sex (e.g., using a numbered list of sexual behaviors so that participants can identify practices by number) could be detailed in a manual.

Ethnography can be used in several ways to enhance *evaluation* of program outcomes. Because of its reliance on assessment within natural contexts, it can be used as a means for developing low inference measures of outcomes, that is, measures that stay close to concrete descriptions of behavior rather than requiring researchers to make judgments or inferences about the nature and meaning of behaviors that they observe. For example, observing participants as they engage in social interactions or simulations of real-life situations in final sessions of the intervention is a more reliable and valid indicator of the impact of the intervention on social interaction skills than is asking participants how they are likely to respond in a social situation through a self-report measure such as a written response to a hypothetical situation. Furthermore, in-depth documentation of the intervention process through the use of participant observation and videotaping has particular utility in efforts to replicate or institutionalize the intervention. Observations are useful in preparing manuals, and tapes can be used to train later facilitators or demonstrate to others "exactly what the intervention looks like" when done effectively.

Ethnography is a very useful tool for facilitating the *involvement of key stakeholders.* Ethnographic methods are geared toward involving stakeholders in data collection through individual and group interviews, and also toward obtaining their views throughout the life of the program. The iterative approach used by ethnographers calls for continuous interaction with stakeholders to obtain both data and analytic or interpretive insights, as well as to provide and gain feedback. In this manner, ethnography ensures that program developers acknowledge the importance of, procure, and sustain the involvement of stakeholders. It also means that stakeholders fully understand all phases of the program and its implementation. *The continual use of ethnographic methods throughout the phases of programming is critical to the continued involvement of stakeholders and, ultimately, to the continuity or institutionalization of the program itself.*

Key point

Finally, *ethnographic data collection throughout the intervention process can help in our efforts to* build theory. For example, the opportunity to examine closely the process of change during the intervention provides data that can be used to modify or extend existing theory or develop new theories. In addition, documentation of how the target phenomenon is manifested in a particular cultural group helps us to build culture-specific theory. Finally, the iterative process involving stakeholders creates the infrastructure for including them not only in program institutionalization, but in theory building to guide culturally-targeted programming in the future.

Key point

NOTES

1. UWASA is a 5-year national research and demonstration project, funded by the Center for Substance Abuse Prevention (HD1-SPO6758), to the Institute for Community Research. Principal Investigator is Jean J. Schensul. Marlene J. Berg serves as co-PI and Project Director. Other members of the multiethnic interdisciplinary team include Mariajosé Romero, PhD, Evaluation Director; Nitza Diaz, Recio Chang, and Essie Hayes, evaluation staff; Donna Owens, Lourdes Hernandéz-Cordova, Graciela Quiñones Rodríguez, Facilitators; and Bonnie Nastasi, PhD, Consultant.

2. The SRPP project was conducted as part of the Women and AIDS Research Program of the International Center for Research on Women as a joint effort of the Center for International Community Health Studies—Connecticut, the Centre for Intersectoral Community Health Studies—Peradeniya (Sri Lanka), and the Institute for Community Research of Hartford, Connecticut. Principal investigators were Stephen Schensul (USA, PI), Jean J. Schensul (USA, co-PI), K. Tudor Silva (Sri Lanka, co-PI), and Priyani Ratnayake (Sri Lanka, co-PI). Other members of the research team included Herbert Aponso (Sri Lanka), M. W. Amarasiri de Silva (Sri Lanka), Merrill Eisenberg (USA), Judy Lewis (USA), Bonnie Nastasi (USA), Chelliah Sivajoganathan (Sri Lanka), and Piyaseeli Wedisinghe (Sri Lanka).

3. Amy Fox, a graduate-level anthropology student from the University of South Florida, conducted this fieldwork on a full-time internship at the ICR from August through December, 1997 for her master's thesis.

4. These assessment tools are examples of materials that can be used during program implementation to collect ethnographic data useful in determining program acceptability and integrity, monitoring individual and group progress over time, and contributing to the understanding of program outcome data.

REFERENCES

Bernard, H. R. (1995). *Research methods in anthropology: Qualitative and quantitative approaches* (2nd ed.). Walnut Creek, CA: AltaMira.

Bernard, H. R. (Ed.). (1998). *Handbook of methods in ethnographic research.* Walnut Creek, CA: AltaMira.

Guisinger, S., & Blatt, S. J. (1994). Individuality and relatedness: Evolution of a fundamental dialectic. *American Psychologist, 49,* 104-111.

Krueger, R. A. (1994). *Focus groups: A practical guide for applied research* (2nd ed.). Thousand Oaks, CA: Sage.

LeCompte, M. D., Millroy, W. L., & Preissle, J. (Eds.). (1992). *The handbook of qualitative research in education.* San Diego, CA: Academic Press.

Lincoln, Y. S., & Guba, E. G. (1985). *Naturalistic inquiry.* Beverly Hills, CA: Sage.

Miles, M. B., & Huberman, A. M. (1994). *Qualitative data analysis* (2nd ed.). Thousand Oaks, CA: Sage.

Morgan, D. L. (1988). *Focus groups as qualitative research.* Newbury Park, CA: Sage.

Morgan, D. L., & Krueger, R. (1998). *The focus group kit.* Thousand Oaks, CA: Sage.

Nastasi, B. K., & Clements, D. H. (1991). Research on cooperative learning: Implications for practice. *School Psychology Review, 20,* 110-131.

Nastasi, B. K., & DeZolt, D. M. (1994). *School interventions for children of alcoholics.* New York: Guilford.

Nastasi, B. K., Schensul, J. J., deSilva, M. W. A., Varjas, K., Silva, K. T., Ratnayake, P., & Schensul, S. L. (1998-1999). Community-based sexual risk prevention program for Sri Lankan youth: Influencing sexual-risk decision making. *International Quarterly of Community Health Education, 18*(1), 139-155.

Nastasi, B. K., Varjas, K., Sarkar, S., & Jayasena, A. (1998). Participatory model of mental health programming: Lessons learned from work in a developing country. *School Psychology Review, 27*(2), 260-276.

Pelto, P. J., & Pelto, G. (1978). *Anthropological research: The structure of inquiry.* New York: Cambridge University Press.

Rogoff, B. (1990). *Apprenticeship in thinking: Cognitive development in social context.* New York: Oxford University Press.

Schensul, S., & Schensul, J. (1978). Advocacy and applied anthropology. In G. Weber & G. McCall (Eds.), *Social scientists as advocates: Views from the applied disciplines.* Beverly Hills, CA: Sage.

Silva, K. T., Schensul, S. L., Schensul, J. J., Nastasi, B. K., de Silva, M. W. A., Sivayoganathan, C., Ratnayake, P., Wedsinghe, P., Lewis, L., Eisenberg, M., & Aponso, H. (1997). *Women and AIDS research program: Youth and sexual risk in Sri Lanka.* Washington, DC: International Center for Research on Women.

Spradley, J. P. (1979). *The ethnographic interview.* New York: Holt, Rinehart & Winston.

Spradley, J. P. (1980). *Participant observation.* New York: Holt, Rinehart & Winston.

Stringer, E. T. (1996). *Action research: A handbook for practitioners.* Thousand Oaks, CA: Sage.

Trotter, R., & Schensul, J. (1998). Applied ethnographic methods. In H. R. Bernard (Ed.), *Handbook of methods in ethnographic research.* Walnut Creek, CA: AltaMira.

Vygotsky, L. S. (1978). *Mind in society: The development of higher psychological processes.* Cambridge, MA: Harvard University Press.

Wertsch, J. V. (1991). *Voices of the mind: A sociocultural approach to mediated action.* Cambridge, MA: Harvard University Press.

APPENDIX A. Observation Protocol, UWASA[4]

Session #:__________ Observer:______________________________ UWASA Session Observation Sheet

Exercise: ____

Activity Time A #:_____ *(minutes)*	*Activity Type*	*Facilitator Technique/Instruction*	**Whole Group Process/Conflict Resolution (if applicable)*
Began	Code	1. Technique: check if technique is used) 2. Rate technique from 0 = not used; 1-4 = if used, from least to most	1. Please check all that apply 2. Then rate from 0-4; 0 = not seen; least characteristic (1) to to most characteristic (4)
________ Ended ________ Total: ________	Group level: _____ Whole* _____ Small _____ Indiv.	RATING modeling: _____ _____ guided - 1 _____ direct - 2 scaffolding: _____ _____ guided - 1 _____ direct - 2 explication: _____ _____ guided - 1 _____ direct - 2 reflection: _____ _____ guided - 1 _____ direct - 2	Whole Group Process Assessment RATING _____ Positive group interdependence _____ _____ Individual accountability _____ _____ Encourage each other _____ _____ Reciprocal sensemaking _____ _____ Cognitive conflict _____ How conflict resolved (overall, ONE ONLY) _____ No resolution _____ Idea dominance _____ Facilitator resolves _____ Idea negotiation _____ Social dominance _____ Idea synthesis

Name and brief description of activity:

X-Site Intervention Type		*X-Site Delivery Method*		*Duration*	
Code	*Type*	*Code*	*Method*	*Code*	*Category*
1	Information (ATOD direct)	1	One on one	1	30 minutes or less
2	Information (ATOD indirect)	2	Didactic	2	31-60 minutes
3	Academic/vocational	3	Supported group interaction	3	61-90 minutes
4	Targeted skills development	4	Experiential	4	91-120 minutes
5	Positive recreation/enrich			5	+120 minutes
6	Emotional/social support				

CODING: You code each session as part of your activities as observer. In terms of the coding format, we are viewing each session in basic time units that are defined by the different activities in which participants will be involved. Activities are initially defined in the curriculum outline for that day's session. Typically, a session begins with the participants arriving, girls will immediately spend 15-20 minutes "having a snack" (a recreational activity), and then facilitators will continue with the rest of the session. Typically, two to three activities are planned each session, however, usually two are completed.

Your session fieldnotes should include a brief rationale, or ethnographic description, of why you coded each activity and method of delivery the way you did, particularly for the UWASA coding scheme. Many of these codes are fuzzy and vague, and I need to be able to follow your logic for the information that you provide.

ETHNOGRAPHIC DESCRIPTIONS: A protocol has been developed in order to provide a general guideline for "things to look for" in your observations and fieldnote write-up. In addition to your fieldnotes, please make sure to fill in the attendance sheets that each facilitator should be completing. Please check to make sure they get filled in properly at the end of each session. Your completed fieldnotes should contain (a) written notes, including follow-up interview/reflection session with the facilitator; (b) completed codesheet; and (c) completed attendance sheet.

APPENDIX B.1. Goals, Objectives, and Exercises Planned and Actually Completed

Session ID: ______________

0.1. Module #:
0.2. Module Goals:

0.3. Session # :
0.4. Session Goals:

0.5. DATE TO BE IMPLEMENTED: Burns School: Wish School:
0.6. ACTUAL DATE: Burns School: Wish School:
0.7. If actual and planned dates differ, please explain why: ______________________________

Module Session	*Curriculum Planned*	*Curriculum Implemented*			
1.1 Exercise #1		1.6 Was exercise implemented? 1. Yes 0. No*	1.8 Were there variations in implementation?		
1.2 Objectives			1.8a Goal	1. Yes*	0. No
1.3 Description			1.8b Description	1. Yes*	0. No
1.4 Materials		1.7 Were objectives achieved? 1. Yes 0. No*	1.8c Materials	1. Yes*	0. No
1.5 Duration			1.8d Duration	1. Yes*	0. No
1.9 Comments: *Please explain all variations and deviations from plans					

APPENDIX B.2. UWASA Facilitator Program Session Information Sheet

MODULE:	
SESSION:	
EXERCISE:	ESTIMATED TIME TO COMPLETE:
OBJECTIVE:	
MATERIALS:	
PREPARATION:	

Context:

Group size:

Actual time:

1. Description of facilitation technique:

    What was facilitated:

    How it was facilitated:

    Girls' response:

    Approximate duration (time) of interactive episode:

2. Description of facilitation technique:

    What was facilitated:

    How it was facilitated:

    Girls' response:

    Approximate duration (time) of interactive episode:

Narrative reflection:

APPENDIX C.1. Activity Log

Instructions:

For each activity, indicate (check the box) the *degree of completion* ("completed," "partially done," "not done"). For activities that are "partially done" or "not done," answer the following questions in the narrative section:

(1) Why was the activity not completed? What happened?

(2) What suggestions do you have for changing the activity for future sessions to make sure that it is completed?

For each activity, also indicate (check the box) the *success* of the activity ("went very well," "OK," "had problems"). For activities that you checked "went very well" or "had problems," describe what happened (what you did as facilitator and what the participants did) and answer the following questions in the narrative section:

(1) If "went very well":

What happened that makes you think the activity went very well?

(2) If "had problems":

Describe the problem.

How did you handle the problem?

How did the group react to the problem and your strategy to address the problem?

If you encounter the problem again, how would you handle it?

Module: ____________________ Unit: ____________________

Activity	*Completed*	*Partially Done*	*Not Done*	*Went Very Well*	*OK*	*Had Problems*

Narrative: (Leave space for narrative here)

APPENDIX C.2. Facilitator Self-Evaluation Checklist

The purposes of the checklist are to (a) facilitate self-monitoring by peer educators and (b) document engagement in specific facilitator behaviors.

_____ I have stated clearly the purpose of the group, my role, and expectations of group members. (FIRST SESSION)
_____ I have established group rules. (FIRST SESSION)
_____ I have stated clearly the objectives of today's session, my role, and expectations of group members.
_____ I have reviewed group rules, as needed.
_____ I have encouraged involvement of all group members (e.g., by structuring group activities, open-ended questioning, asking each member to contribute ideas).
_____ I have encouraged group members to express ideas, feelings, attitudes.
_____ I have encouraged group members to consider each others' viewpoints.
_____ I have facilitated knowledge acquisition (e.g., by conducting relevant activities, providing information).
_____ I have facilitated debunking of myths (e.g., by encouraging or providing alternative views).
_____ I have facilitated attitude change (e.g., through discussion, confrontation of perspectives).
_____ I have facilitated use of problem solving (e.g., teaching or guiding practice of problem solving).
_____ I have facilitated development of individual plans for engaging in healthy behavior.
_____ Before the close of the session, I reviewed what we learned.
_____ I facilitated self-evaluation and discussion of group process.

APPENDIX C.3 Group Process Self-Evaluation

DIRECTIONS: Each group member answers Questions 1 to 5 (Circle the appropriate response).

Yes No 1. Did all group members participate?
Yes No 2. Did you encourage each other to express ideas or opinions?
Yes No 3. Were different ideas or opinions expressed?
Yes No 4. Did you discuss different ideas or opinions and try to reach agreement?
Yes No 5. Did group members have specific roles?

What were the roles?
_____ recorder
_____ reporter
_____ other ____

As a group, discuss and answer Questions 6 and 7.

Yes No 6. Did the group work well together?
Yes No 7. How could you improve the group process? (list ideas)

APPENDIX D. Pre-Post Measure of Sexual Risk Decision Making, SRPP

Read the following story (personal dilemma) and answer the questions that follow.

> You are engaged to be married. Your partner is trying to convince you to have vaginal intercourse with withdrawal before ejaculation. He/she claims this will prevent pregnancy. In addition, your partner claims that he/she is a virgin and thus there is no reason to be concerned about transmission of STDs or AIDS.

What risks are involved? [risks]

How might you protect yourself against these risks? [protection against risks]

What would you do in this situation? Why? [proposed actions]

How confident do you feel that you could protect yourself against personal risks in this situation? (check one) [level of confidence] Explain your level of confidence (e.g., Why do you feel very confident?) [confidence]

________ Very confident
________ Somewhat confident
________ Confident enough
________ Minimally confident
________ Not confident at all

SCORING CRITERIA FOR SEXUAL RISK DECISION-MAKING RESPONSES

RISK

1. Accuracy in identification of risk? (accurate = 1; inaccurate = 0)
2. Type of risk(s) mentioned? (coded for categories: pregnancy = 1; loss of virginity = 2; STDs/AIDS = 3; loss of relationship = 4; coercion = 5; loss of marriageability or social status = 6; promiscuity = 7; failure to withdraw = 8)

PROTECTION

1. Accuracy? (accurate = 1; inaccurate = 0)
2. Type of protection mentioned? (coded for categories: condom = 1; avoid penetration = 2; avoid sex = 3; single partner = 4; communicate or negotiate with partner = 5; safe sex = 6; get information from a medical professional = 7)

PROPOSED ACTION

1. Accuracy re: protection? (accurate = 1; inaccurate = 0)
2. Type of action? (coded for categories: negotiate with partner = 1; use condom = 2; abstinence = 3; nonpenetrative/safe sex = 4; consult with medical professional or seek advice = 5; end the relationship = 6)

LEVEL OF CONFIDENCE/EXPLANATION

Level: Very confident = 1; Somewhat confident = 2; Confident enough = 3;
Minimally confident = 4; Not confident at all = 5.

EXPLANATION

Is it realistic/reasonable (i.e., is the level of confidence logical given the nature of the proposed action)? (realistic/reasonable = 1; unrealistic/unreasonable = 0)

2

USING ETHNOGRAPHY TO INFLUENCE PUBLIC POLICY

G. Alfred Hess, Jr.

INTRODUCTION

Case Study

The 3-inch high headline of the afternoon edition of the *Chicago Sun Times* screamed: "Dropouts At Nearly 50%!" Never before had the Chicago Panel on Public School Policy, on which I served as Executive Director, been able to generate so much coverage for one of our policy-relevant research reports, even though we released more than 35 of them during the Panel's 15-year existence. Our timing was right; it was major news, and nothing else had happened that day. The related story carried the essential points of our report: Forty-three percent of entering students dropped out of the Chicago Public Schools, but at different schools, rates ranged from 11% to 63% (Hess & Lauber, 1985). These points all had been carefully summarized in a listing of major findings and recommendations in the front of the report.

In a city in which the Board of Education had been saying the dropout rate was 8%, our report was real news. It was even more newsworthy because the Board of Education had cooperated in the study, the study used the Board's own data, and the Board did not dispute the accuracy of the numbers. After 5 years of charges by advocacy groups and denials by General Superintendents (three different ones), the dropout problem was finally acknowledged to be real and massive.

A year and a half later, the Chicago Panel released a matched-pairs ethnographic study of eight Chicago high schools (Hess, Wells, Prindle, Kaplan, & Liffman, 1986). The high schools were matched for types and preparation of entering students but differed significantly on dropout rates. We wanted to highlight what was different about the more successful high schools. In the process, we discovered one of the reasons that all students were less successful in Chicago schools compared to the suburbs: They were being shortchanged in terms of actual instructional time provided. Each classroom period was, on average, 8 minutes shorter than those of their suburban peers (representing one period less per week, 20%, for each major subject) and their theoretically 300 minutes of instruction per day were being shortened by nonexistent study halls at the beginning and end of the day. We called the study, *"Where's Room 185?" How Schools Can Reduce Their Dropout Problem.* At the press conference called to release the report, we explained that Room 185, the assignment on students' schedules at DuSable High School for first and last period study halls, did not exist.

That afternoon, Channel 2 reporter Dorothy Tucker visited DuSable, a school in the African American-dominated heart of the city. Tucker, a Black woman, was not allowed in the school, but she interviewed students leaving school early, who explained for the camera that although they were assigned to study hall, they knew they were supposed to go home early. On the 5 o'clock news, Tucker and the news announcer interviewed the Board of Education president and me, following the videotape showing the students leaving the school. The president said, "We respect CHIPs (the Chicago Panel's acronym); they always do careful research. We'll investigate, and if we find it to be true, things will change." The next summer, the elderly woman who had been the ineffective titular principal at DuSable High School took early retirement. In the meantime, the General Superintendent derided the Chicago Panel for "trashing"[1] the city's schools. The city's papers both editorialized that it was a scandal for the school system to shortchange its students so shabbily. The Superintendent responded in a Letter to the Editor that city schools could not be expected to do any better, because they had such a preponderance of disadvantaged students to educate. This acrimonious exchange moved school reform a step closer to realization.

During the 1989 annual meeting of the American Anthropological Association in Washington, DC, I was invited to present testimony to a subcommittee of the U.S. House of Representatives Committee on Education and Labor. The Elementary, Secondary, and Vocational Education Subcommittee was considering H.R. 3347, a bill to establish a National Demonstration Program for Educational Performance Agreements for School Restructuring. I testified in favor of the bill, which was sponsored by a Republican congressman from Vermont.

When I returned from the Capitol building to attend the annual meetings, anthropologists were complaining that the work of anthropology is generally overlooked and specifically ignored when public policy is formulated. They claimed that other disciplines were more frequently sought out to present testimony to legislatures and to give interviews to the media. Some anthropologists were offended by this lack of recognition. Others, particularly staff representing the Association itself, appeared defensive about their own seeming lack of effectiveness. In my view, ethnographers were having limited success in the policy-making arena because they paid little careful attention to the role of testimony in the making of public policy and did not have a clear understanding of what "news" is, and to whom the media look for expert comment.

On another occasion, when I was testifying in U.S. Federal District Court, the judge interrupted me to ask why I thought it was important to a decision about desegregation in the St. Louis Public Schools that students were achieving better than they had previously but were still not close to reaching national test norms. In answering, I pointed out that 60% of white parents were avoiding enrolling their students in the St. Louis Public Schools; that if those students were enrolled, there would be enough white students in the system to integrate all of the city's schools, not just half of them; and that to attract these nonparticipating white students, city residents would have to believe that all the city schools were of top quality. Presentation of these data helped the judge understand for the first time the connection between desegregation, student achievement, and white flight from urban school systems in the United States.

These incidents illustrate some of the issues related to ensuring that serious attention is paid to policy-relevant research in the media, the legislature, and the courts. Most important is that the researcher has to present good research that is relevant to policies of current interest to the general public or issues before a court. Once policymakers know about the existence of a relevant research base, they will be more likely to pay close attention to it for information about a wider range of policy concerns. Researchers *can* establish a role as policy analysts who are called upon by the press, legislators, and lawyers, if that role is based on locally respected research that is presented by the researcher in a form that can be readily used by the media, policymakers, or the courts.

SETTING THE POLICY AGENDA

On rare occasions, research begun for theoretical reasons becomes relevant to policy issues discussed in the media, legislative bodies, or the courts. It is, however, relatively unusual for research designed to answer theoretical questions to be particularly effective in shaping solutions to policy debates. More frequently, effective policy research starts out with a focus on a policy-relevant problem and then develops knowledge that will help to resolve the related policy issue.

Shaping Policy-Relevant Research

Issues Critical to Shaping Policy-Relevant Research

- Framing the problem, and
- Finding a "hook" or lure that will ensure that your research is recognized
- Knowing which funding sources will support your research
- Establishing a target audience of policymakers or other decision makers

Framing the problem and finding a "hook." The first step in engaging in a policy-oriented research project is finding a direction or a focus. Hooks or angles that appeal to policymakers are especially important when searching for a direction.

They are what gain the support of funders and those who control access to the data or field site for the research. They also convince others that the research will produce valuable information by relating it to current or potential policy issues that are important to a target audience—a local community where the research is conducted, a city council, or a state or national legislature or court.

EXAMPLE 2.1

TWO APPROACHES TO FINDING A HOOK FOR FRAMING THE PROBLEM OF SCHOOL REFORM

When the Chicago Panel was proposing to study the dropout problem in the Chicago Public Schools, a public debate existed about the effectiveness of the city's schools. The school system was recovering from a fiscal bankruptcy; in response, for the first time, the mayor appointed a primarily minority Board of Education, which selected the first black superintendent of schools in the city's history. As fiscal stability was being forcibly imposed upon the system by the state legislature as a condition of financial assistance, some citizens, including members of the board of the Chicago Panel, began to ask why fiscal stability was so significant. Was it enough for the school system to be financially sound if its students were not being properly educated?

The key question, then, was how to document whether the school system was properly educating its students. At the time, two organizations in Chicago had developed some policy-relevant educational research expertise: the Chicago Panel, a newcomer to the policy research scene, and a well-established older center, Designs for Change. The two groups independently chose complementary ways to frame the problem of school effectiveness and used different hooks to gain support and attention for their research. The Chicago Panel decided to determine how many entering ninth graders either eventually graduated from, or dropped out of, each high school in the city. Our hook was to try to establish a cost associated with each student who left the city's schools prior to graduation. The staff at Designs for Change (1985) set out to show what proportion of the graduating class could read at national norms. Their hook was that the outcome almost certainly would be well under 50% because the national norm, by definition, was the score below which half of the nation's 12th graders would achieve. Both hooks were used successfully to secure funding support for the research projects, and both received extensive media attention when the reports were released early in 1985.

Finding the appropriate funding source. Funding sources can shape research and policy. Most policy-relevant researchers recognize that successful research efforts require knowing which funders are available, how to approach them, and what they will fund. Potential sources of funds include philanthropic foundations, corporate sponsors, and government grants or contracts. University-based researchers can often seek start-up research funds from their universities, from graduate or postgraduate fellowships, from university grants for new professors, or from their research foundations.

Having prior knowledge of the potential funder's interests, past history of funding, and approach to problems is an important element in framing the problem and determining the hook. The better the fit between the funder's interests and the researcher's approach, the more likely it is that the project will be funded. On some occasions, the funder might approach the researcher, such as in litigation, when lawyers approach a researcher to provide an expert's report or testimony, or in instances where a foundation is interested in mounting a specific program that the researcher is recognized as being able to carry out. On other occasions, a school system or other organization might request and provide funding for an evaluation of part of its program. In such cases, problems are already framed, and hooks are not needed.

Establishing the target audience. It is very important to establish the target audience(s) for the research report. When lawyers hire a researcher to appear as an expert witness, the audience will be the judge or jury. If the government grants a contract for research, it usually also specifies the intended audience. When an independent researcher or research organization is shaping the policy research, the target might be community actors or policymakers (either legislators or administrators), or the public, via the media. Establishing the target audience for the research is closely connected to framing the problem, finding the hook, and knowing the sources of support. The definition of the problem might be quite different if the target audience is a judge, a school superintendent, a board of education, or the news media. Shaping policy-relevant research is an interaction between each of these four elements: problem definition, hook, sources of support, and target audience.

Designing Research Projects

Cross Reference: See Books 1 and 2 for other issues related to research design

Research projects are organized around well-framed policy problems. When the Chicago Panel determined the scope of the dropout problem in Chicago, we also found that the higher the proportion of entering freshmen in a school who read below grade level or who were a year or more older than normal, the higher the dropout rate would be for a school. The new problem, then, was whether schools could do anything about reducing the dropout rate, given that most public high schools had little control over the age or reading preparation of those who came to the school to enroll. Some schools did establish achievement levels for admittance; for example, Lane Technical High School required seventh-grade marks of "B" or better for admission. Other schools in more middle-class neighborhoods limited entrance of low-achieving students from outside the neighborhood. But most city high schools enrolled all students from their neighborhoods who could not gain admission to more selective schools. We wanted to know if, given the students who enrolled, schools could do anything to improve their graduation rates.

To investigate this problem, we looked for pairs of schools that had similar student enrollment characteristics, where one had a higher than expected, and the other a lower than expected, dropout rate. By establishing four matched pairs of high schools, each pair with similar students but different dropout rates, we could hypothesize that something different was happening in the better performing schools. Using identical ethnographic methods in each school, we could look for practices and patterns in the schools that might account for the differences. Comparing results across four pairs of schools, we would look for similarities in practice that distinguished better performing from less well-performing schools regardless of the preparation level of the entering students.[2]

The four pairs of schools constituted 8 of the 64 high schools in the city. They represented the whole range of student enrollment characteristics (preparation, race/ethnicity, socioeconomic status), so we could argue that our results would be representative of the whole city and generally applicable to urban high schools in large cities across the United States. Because we wanted to mobilize large-scale public support for improving the city's schools, we chose not to promise confidentiality to the participating schools so that the press could confirm our results. We did extend confidentiality to individual teachers and students who were interviewed or observed in class.

We selected four ethnographic field-workers, each of whom spent 2 months in each school of a pair, alternating their time over a 4-month period. We developed common interview protocols and a list of the types of people to be interviewed, a randomizing strategy for selecting the individuals to be interviewed, and a class observation schedule. We also established weekly meetings for internal reporting, procedure checking, and agenda setting. These were the key elements in designing the research project that we called *"Where's Room 185?" How Schools Can Reduce Their Dropout Problem* (Hess et al., 1986).

Cross Reference: See Book 1 on designing and conducting ethnographic research

Cross Reference: See Book 2 for using quantitative and qualitative data in an ethnographic study

As Book 1 of the **Ethnographer's Toolkit** makes clear, a critical step in designing a research project is to choose research methods that will provide appropriate information about the problem being investigated. For those projects, the Chicago Panel used a mix of qualitative, or descriptive, and quantitative data, or enumerable.

To establish the dropout rate in each high school, we used a quantitative approach that examined more than 33,000 individual student records for each of three consecutive cohorts of students (the Classes of 1982, 1983, and 1984). We analyzed the data primarily through descriptive cross-tabulations and later examined the data in more depth through the use of regression analyses. The descriptive data allowed us to assert a dropout rate for the entire city high school system and for each individual school in the system, whereas the regression analyses allowed us to determine which characteristics of students accounted for the level of the dropout rate.[3] Later, we would use a similar approach to ascribe dropout rates to each elementary school in the system on the basis of the eventual success or failure of their eighth-grade graduates. However, when we wanted to know which practices were more successful in enabling higher proportions of students to graduate from high school, we adopted more ethnographic approaches involving interviewing, classroom observation, and participant observation in the life of the school to supplement quantitative data such as absence rates, class cutting, and course failure rates.

Definition: Outliers were schools whose dropout rates were significantly above or below the mean.

We next had to determine which sites or data sources to investigate. In our matched-pairs ethnographic study of eight high schools, we chose schools that were **outliers** from the general regression line relating dropout rates to student preparation.[4] We also chose pairs of schools in different contexts and at different levels of dropping out. We looked at two high schools with predominantly African American students; two with predominantly Hispanic American students; two with proportionately larger numbers of Euro-

American students (at that point, there were no high schools with majority Caucasian student bodies); and two selective vocational high schools that chose their students on the basis of prior achievement levels.

One important aspect of designing policy-relevant research is deciding how much emphasis to place on generalizability and how much to place on specificity. Because we wanted to be able to generalize to schools across the city, we sought as sites schools that were geographically dispersed and that represented the city's range of socioeconomic conditions. At the same time, we were looking for a richness of detail and specificity about practices related to dropping out that we could achieve only by focusing on some (in this case an eighth) of the city's high schools, not all of them. By contrast, when we were establishing the dropout rates, we needed and reported on data from every school so that we could accurately gauge the universe of student outcomes in the city.

The design also had to weigh the advantages of offering confidentiality to our informants against the advantage of verifiability that would accompany identifying the sites we investigated. In *"Where's Room 185?"* we sought to balance these concerns by not keeping our sites confidential, but also by not revealing which interviewee provided which reported response or comment. This had the advantage of allowing the media to visit the schools we had investigated to confirm for their readers what we were reporting while still protecting individual teachers or students from reprisal by principals or administrators who might have been embarrassed by the report.

Cross Reference:
See Books 1and 6 for information on the rights of research subjects to protection of their privacy and confidentiality

However, when we later set out to study 14 representative schools that were implementing the Chicago School Reform Act of 1988, we knew that we would be working in these schools for 5 years and making a number of interim reports. We felt it was important to guarantee anonymity to the schools so that we could report honestly on the problems being encountered without losing access to the sites. Many times, we revisited this decision as reporters and funders called to ask for the names of the successful schools on which we had reported. We had been so worried about protecting the schools with problems that we did not realize that anonymity denied recognition to the schools that were successful—an issue we had not anticipated!

Cross Reference: See Book 1 for a discussion of how logistical and resource considerations constrain research design

Two other components of our research design involved establishing the staffing pattern and the timeline for the project. For the matched-pairs high school study, we had very limited resources, but we needed ethnographers who could work full-time for a short period. We had to compress the time line so that most of the staff were employed for only 5 months. For our school reform implementation study (Hess, 1996), we were able to raise far more money, so we could use a larger staff for a 6-year period, although many worked only part-time each week. For this study, we were able to use graduate students who worked only 2 or 3 days per week but did so for 6 years with the supervision and coordination of full-time staff. In the former study, we were trying to identify persistent patterns of behavior in a stable organizational context. Thus, a concentrated study at one point in time sufficed. In the latter study, we wanted to understand processes of change; that required a longer time period but was less intense.

To summarize, critical issues in considering ethnographic design in policy research include the following:

- Timing (Will the study be conducted in the appropriate period of time to have an effect on decision making?)
- Staffing (Can sufficient competent staff be hired to guarantee that the study will be both rigorous and cost-effective?)
- Sampling (Is there an appropriate balance between generalizability and specificity? Is sample size large or representative enough to be convincing to the audience for the research?)

- Data collection (Are data collection techniques appropriate for the task, and does the design involve both qualitative and quantitative data collection?)

Finally, it is important to consider the role of theory in policy research. In policy research, the research problem is driven by the situation, the stakeholders, and the decisions to be made rather than the specific research interests of the researcher. However, the results (e.g., explanations uncovered for differences among schools) stem from findings organized into explanatory theories. Thus, policy research is not absent theory; rather, theories emerge or are drawn upon to explain findings that guide directions for policy change.[5]

Securing Financial Support

Steps in Securing Financial Support

- Draft an initial proposal stating your problem, describing what you plan to do, and indicating how much it will cost.
- Obtain the funding agency's guidelines for proposal submission and schedule of proposal due dates.
- Make an informal inquiry to determine if the target agency is interested in your project.
- Submit a completed research proposal.
- Revise your proposal if required by the agency.
- Confirm your agreements with funders if they agree to support you.

As indicated earlier, the level of support available for a particular policy-relevant research project will have important implications for the scope of the research project. Correspondingly, the scale of the envisioned project may change the type of sponsorship sought for the project. For our matched-pairs ethnographic study, we sought follow-up funding from the same foundation that had provided funds for our initial study documenting the dropout rate for every Chicago high school. Because the foundation's staff had indicated that we might expect a similar grant of about $35,000, we knew we had to fit the research design to those limitations. On the other hand, when we were designing the 14-school reform monitoring project, we knew the scope of the research would require much more extensive work over a prolonged period. So, we designed a funding scheme that would solicit support from a number of foundations that would either consider multiple-year support or would invite recurring proposals on an annual basis. In this instance, the relationship between the scope of the project and the sources of support needed to be interactive.

The first step in securing support is to draft a proposal or a prospectus that describes the problem being investigated, the research being proposed, the methods to be used, the staff to be employed, the time line envisioned, and the projected costs and the share of those costs being requested from each funder. Most of the research conducted by the Chicago Panel has been supported by philanthropic foundations that were willing to accept proposals on a recurring schedule and whose way of operating was to negotiate the format for the proposal with us (i.e., the proposal was tailored for the foundation with the help of foundation staff). Sometimes, however, we have submitted applications for competitively awarded grants or contracts. In cases of competition, the format of the proposal is usually carefully spelled out by the granting agency (frequently, these are arms of the state or federal government). Even less often, we have been requested to submit a proposed research agenda for a specific purpose, such as to provide information to a court as part of a specific litigation.

In each situation, choosing the appropriate funding agency is key to securing support. If the foundation is not interested in the general area that the proposal addresses, the grantwriter will not be able to frame the proposal successfully. Sometimes, multiple funders are asked to fund the same program, especially when it involves a large initiative. Even when multiple funders jointly support the same initiative, it is important to design individual proposals to speak to the specific interests of each.

Some foundations might be willing to support only a specific part of the overall project. For example, the research-oriented Spencer Foundation provided the bulk of our funding for examining changes in student achievement under the Chicago Reform Act, whereas the Fry Foundation, the Chicago Community Trust, and the Woods Charitable Fund were more interested in supporting the ethnographic work required to document successful implementation practices in the 14 observed schools.

The process of securing foundation support for a proposal generally follows a common pattern. The first step is to obtain and explore the foundation's guidelines for proposal submission and its schedule of proposal due dates. Generally, this is followed with an informal inquiry to staff of the foundation to discover whether they would be interested in receiving such a proposal. Some foundations require this to be a more formal submission in the form of a letter of inquiry. If the response is positive, the next stage is submission of the proposal itself, with all of the necessary supporting documentation that demonstrates that the requesting organization meets the required conditions to receive a grant. The proposal will be assigned to a specific staff person, usually known as a program officer. After reviewing the proposal and preparing a series of questions to solicit further information about the proposed project (i.e., the kind of information that staff officers know members of the foundation's board will want before making a funding decision), the program officer will usually conduct a site visit with the organization and lead project researcher.

During the site visit, the funder may raise important questions that uncover problems in the proposal or reveal specific interests that might be addressed more effectively in the grant proposal. When this occurs, the applicant frequently will be encouraged to redraft the proposal to address these issues more carefully. The modification process presents particular problems for the research team. In some cases, the modification does not affect the substance of the proposed research and simply stands to enhance the likelihood of funding. Such modifications are not problematic. In other cases, the interests of the potential funder and of the researcher may be far enough apart to raise serious questions about whether or not to submit the proposal at all.

After the proposal review and site visit, a staff person will prepare a summary of the proposal and a recommendation about whether to grant funding, and if so, at what level. In larger foundations, this recommendation may have to go through a staff review process first; in smaller foundations, the recommendation may go directly to members of the board. Most foundations have established an annual schedule for reviewing grants, often considering specific arenas of grant-making at different meetings in the year (e.g., education might be considered in the fall, culture and arts in the winter, community services in the spring, etc.).

If your proposal is accepted and a grant is made to support the research project, you will be asked to confirm in writing your willingness to accept the grant and its accompanying conditions. Generally, these conditions restrict the use of the grant to the purposes articulated in your proposal, assure the grantor that you do meet the criteria for organizations qualified to receive grants from the funder, and indicate your willingness to meet the reporting requirements of the foundation, including both accounting for the use of the funds and demonstrating the successful conclusion of the research project.

Conducting the Research

Conducting policy-relevant research is not very different from conducting theoretical, or researcher-driven, research. In both cases, you have a question you need to answer, a set of methods you have chosen to employ, a site/set of sites/data source you have decided would produce important information in answering your question, a set of time and personnel opportunities and constraints, and just plain hard work to do. There are, however, some unique aspects to conducting policy-relevant research.

Gaining site access may be quite different for policy-relevant researchers. If the researcher is well-known as a policy researcher, site **gatekeepers** may respond quite differently from the way they might respond to other, non-policy-oriented researchers. The sites where theoretical research is done are likely to remain anonymous to protect informants' privacy. Thus, the potential for embarrassment in these sites is low, but there are some specifiable costs in terms of the perception of the researchers as intrusive and inconvenient. Furthermore, programs found by researchers to be exemplary may not be recognized because of the confidentiality rule. Schools can negotiate with researchers for some offsetting benefits to compensate for the inconvenience incurred by the research (e.g., payment of a stipend to those interviewed, or designing an aspect of the research to answer a specific question of the site managers).

Definition: Gatekeepers are people who control access to a site, population, or group, or to information

In policy-relevant research, the potential for recognition or embarrassment is much higher, but the site managers also may be interested in the outcomes of the research for their own purposes. Thus, when the Consortium on Chicago School Research, a collaborative of Chicago-based researchers, conducts surveys of teachers or students, it provides an individual school profile of survey results for every school with a 50% return rate, while refusing to identify publicly any individual schools (their studies are reported in Bryk, Easton, Kerbow, Rollow, & Sebring, 1993; Easton et al., 1991). This acts as both an incentive to boost response rates and a benefit to school leaders, who can use the information to plan improvement. Similarly, when the Chicago Panel negotiated access to the 14 schools we tracked through the initial implementation of the 1988 Chicago School Reform Act (Hess, 1996), to encourage their participation we promised to provide feedback to each school on what we were observing and how that school compared with others we were observing. We also constructed our interim reports to encourage schools to change unsuccessful practices; in doing so, we were adopting a critical ethnographic approach. By contrast, when we set out to do the matched-pairs ethnographic study in eight high schools, the school system was still very centralized in its operations. Participation could be assured simply by convincing the Deputy Superintendent that the results would be beneficial to the school system. He then called the eight principals in our target sites and directed them to participate.

Cross Reference: See Book 1 for a discussion of critical theory and its influence on design

Once researchers have gained access and willingness of site managers to participate in a study, they must implement what they promised to do in their proposals and access agreements. Although it may strike the reader as strange to advocate that researchers keep their promises, many researchers, unfortunately, do not. They may have promised to do more than they could deliver, particularly in large-scale, competitively awarded research, such as that funded by government contracts. Promising too much is a practice that endangers future funding, particularly if the researcher repeats the pattern. Of course, conditions in the field may require modifications in the research design, which can be negotiated with funders. Most funders are sympathetic to changes in design if they can be justified.

Cross Reference: See Book 1, Chapters 4 and 5, for a more detailed description of the formulation and adaptation of research designs

One major difference between conducting problem-oriented policy-relevant research and doing research driven by researcher interests is that to be relevant to decision makers, ***the research must be timely,*** in terms of both the problem it addresses and the actionable time lines of the target policymakers. The potential witness whose research is incomplete as the trial begins is the expert witness who is unlikely to be contacted a second time. Similarly, policy research that is not completed until after the legislature has adjourned or enacted an alternative solution fails the test of timeliness. The necessity of timeliness forces hard choices on researchers. Complicated and time-consuming analyses, however interesting they might be, can lead to long delays in completing research projects that could have devastating effects. Delayed results may mean that other, less carefully conducted research with inaccurate results may gain wider circulation and become the basis for misguided policy-setting. Delays can also exhaust financial support for the project prior to the completion of the research. In such cases, future funding may become unavailable from the same sponsor, who will not make a new grant until the final report on the previous grant is completed.

Key point

Another aspect of policy-relevant research is ***keeping people whom you eventually hope to influence abreast of your activities.*** Policy-relevant research is most effective when the press is anxiously awaiting the results of your current project. In the case of litigation research, sharing early results or indications of results may be critical to the development of the strategy being developed by a legal team. By keeping others abreast of their efforts, researchers establish expectations that produce greater receptivity to research results.

Key point

Planned research may produce surprises as well as anticipated results. When the Chicago Panel was conducting research in matched pairs of high schools, we set out to discover why some high schools had lower dropout rates than others. We successfully completed that research and duly reported the findings in our report. However, we also uncovered important information that helped to explain why dropout rates in most Chicago high schools were high when compared to the dropout rates for high schools in suburban areas. In particular, we uncovered information about how the management of resources and personnel in the school system had negative effects on Chicago students.

The quandary we faced was whether to ignore this unanticipated information and simply report the data we had originally sought (and told our sponsors and the managers of the school system we were seeking) or to adjust our reporting and include this other, more explosive, information. Because our overriding interest in conducting the research was to discover information that would improve the educational opportunities for children in Chicago, we decided to include the controversial information in our final report and to focus attention on this component of our research. Thus, the catchy part of the title of the report, "*Where's Room 185?*" was designed as a hook for the media to focus reporters' attention on management practices in all of the high schools that were short changing the city's youth. However, it was the inclusion of this information, and the decision to focus attention on it rather than on the comparative findings that we also reported, that incurred the ire of the General Superintendent and led to his charge that we were "trashing" the Chicago Public Schools.

TARGETING THE PUBLIC

The best policy-relevant research is useless unless others, particularly those who make policy, know of your results and understand the recommendations that flow from them. The following sections of this chapter examine methods of disseminating and reporting on policy-relevant research. The first section discusses strategies and tactics to draw public attention to policy-relevant research, primarily through the media. Next, I examine the process of bringing such research directly to the attention of policymakers through testimony presented in various policy-setting venues. The final section of the chapter describes one highly specialized form of presenting testimony—being an expert witness in litigation.

Types of Media Coverage of Policy-Relevant Research

Six Important Types of Media Coverage for Policy-Relevant Research[6]

- Self-initiated coverage, such as a press conference or release of a study
- Letters to the editor
- Editorial comment
- Analysis of breaking news
- "React" coverage
- Deep background

Press conferences, press releases, and other self-initiated coverage. These are the most typical forms of coverage for the release of policy-relevant research. Their format and logistics are quite standard, and any press guide can provide additional details. At minimum, *press alerts* must be sent out to attract the press to a press conference or news event. A *press statement* must be prepared. The *prepared remarks* of those making the announcements must be available. A meeting room has to be set up in a fashion helpful to the media. You will need the following: tables for the print media to take notes, camera spots for TV (with good sight lines and a carefully considered background), and a table or rostrum for microphones for good sound recording for radio and television. The findings and recommendations of the study have to be carefully summarized and presented in

Cross Reference:
See Book 3 on the logistics of setting up focused group interviews, which have guidelines similar to press conferences

an easily accessible manner. These must have a "policy hook" that links the study to issues in which the public is interested.

EXAMPLE 2.2

MAXIMIZING MEDIA INTEREST IN A PRESS CONFERENCE

The press conference for the release of *"Where's Room 185?"* was scheduled early in the morning; we wanted the media to have time to get to various schools afterwards to expand their coverage with reaction pieces to confirm our findings and perhaps heighten interest by engendering opposition to our findings. As described earlier, nothing could have created more publicity than when the reporter, Dorothy Tucker, was not allowed into DuSable High School. Had she been admitted, her camera shots would have shown students at desks in classrooms where they are supposed to be; her pictures would have overwhelmed her "voice-over" comments that the study said these students were being shortchanged. Instead, her video showed students ducking out of school, just as we had reported, and the pictures and words reinforced our veracity! What could the president of the Board of Education do but agree to investigate?

The hook in this story was that the mayor had convened an Education Summit only a few months earlier to explore ways of improving the city's schools. While the school superintendent was participating in the summit, his regular line was, "What else can we do? It's the kids who are at fault." He regularly trotted out his own life story (i.e., "poor black kid raised on rural farm rises to school superintendent!") as an example that these kids could make it, too, if they would just try as hard as he did. However, our study showed that the superintendent could no longer just blame the victims (Ryan, 1976); although poverty was a tremendous problem, the school system itself was doing things that made success less likely for Chicago students.

Voice of the people

State turned its back on poor students

CHICAGO—The State of Illinois has turned its back on the disadvantaged. That is the conclusion we reached as we examined the pattern of school funding in Illinois over the last two decades. As members of the EdEquity Coalition, we compiled these figures for the recently released report, "The Inequity in Illinois School Finance."

In 1973, there were 319,000 low-income students in Illinois public schools, just 13.8 percent of the enrollment. By 1989, there were more than 500,000 (27.8 percent). Thus, nearly 200,000 formerly middle-income children have fallen into poverty during the last two decades.

In addition, the spread of poverty has been statewide. In the past, Chicago was home to the predominant number of poor children in Illinois. In 1973, only four school districts in this six-county metropolitan area enrolled as many as a quarter of their students from economically disadvantaged families, and there were only 43 such districts downstate. By 1989, there were 35 metropolitan area districts and 192 downstate districts with at least a quarter of their students coming from low-income families.

How did the state respond to this growing poverty in our midst? It turned its back. Between 1970 and 1976, the state share of the cost of education rose from 32 percent of all costs to more than 48 percent. During the following six years, the share fell back to 38 percent.

This forced the burden of funding schools back on local school districts. Wealthy school districts did not mind. But the school districts enrolling large numbers of low-income children were also districts with little property wealth, and they could not make up for the state's declining support. Only in Chicago, with its tremendous property wealth boom, did local revenues keep pace with suburban growth. Thus, it was primarily south suburban and downstate schools enrolling the state's poorest children that were left underfunded by the state's neglect.

But in addition to neglect, the state acted directly to take money away from school districts serving these most disadvantaged students. In 1978 and again in 1982, the General Assembly changed the school aid formula to reduce the cap on the number of low-income students school districts could use to qualify for compensatory state support. In 1973, when these compensatory funds (State Chapter I) were first included in the aid formula, a district could count 75 percent of its low-income students. At that time, only Chicago was limited by the cap. Now, only 62.5 percent of students can be counted, and 19 other school districts—all of which have higher concentrations of low-income students than does Chicago—are also denied full support.

Chicago school reform was targeted to bring improvements to city schools with heavy concentrations of low-income students. Now the Board of Education's fiscal crisis, as recently reported by the Tribune, leads some to suggest taking away these compensatory funds aimed at helping those students who need the most help.

Not investing in the futures of poor young people means reaping a reward of high costs in welfare, crime and taxes, as our 1985 study of dropouts showed. We citizens must arouse ourselves and tell our legislators to reverse the actions of previous General Assemblies. We must correct the inequities in school funding, and we must do it now.

G. Alfred Hess Jr.
Executive director
Chicago Panel on Public School Policy and Finance

Figure 2.1. An op-ed piece.

Letters to the editor/editorial replies. A second approach to coverage of studies relevant to current policy debates is to submit letters to the editor or op-ed pieces to local or national newspapers. Figure 2.1 is one such op-ed piece on a study released by the Chicago Panel in 1991.

Key point

The key to success for letters to the editor and op-ed pieces is timing and format. Short letters generally will be carried with many others in the general letters part of the editorial page. Frequently, only representative letters will get published. Many papers have a specialized space for lengthier and more cogently argued responses. Op-ed pieces must be tightly argued and normally cannot exceed 300 words.

The radio/television version of letters to the editor is an editorial reply. In the United States, most stations run editorials that express the views of the management of the station. Then, they make response time available. These are usually tightly managed but relatively accessible to the public. Chicago radio and television stations now require that the reply be submitted in advance to ensure that it conforms to the 1-minute time limit for taping. Radio and television have the advantage of reaching much wider audiences than the editorial page of a newspaper, but they have a far briefer message; they also schedule news coverage only at certain hours. For that reason, researchers must be aware of whether or not the desired audiences actually will be listening or watching when the editorial and its reply are broadcast. For example, Chicago television stations have moved their news coverage to early in the afternoon. This means that people who work in the afternoon, such as the policy-making audience I am trying to reach, can no longer watch the news. As a consequence, I have virtually stopped contributing editorial replies.

Editorial comment. Putting your own words on the editorial pages or on the news is important, but it is much more helpful when media managers will support your findings and recommendations. Your research then gains added weight because it has convinced those who regularly produce the news and follow the policy issues that you are addressing. Infrequently, editorial writers will simply be won over by the cogency of your research, the timeliness of its release, and the importance of the issues. At other times, such as at the release of "*Where's Room 185?*", the reaction of major actors in the policy arena (in this case, the superintendent of the school system) will prompt the managing editors to respond and add their support to your point. More regularly, researchers solicit editorial comment with a direct request for support of a report being released. In a large media market such as Chicago, these requests are called "making the rounds of the editorial boards"; they entail setting up a joint interview with several editors at each newspaper or station.

Analysis of breaking news. When major school news stories break, the media both report the news and seek to help the public understand that news. As policy researchers show that they are knowledgeable about events in the public eye and can successfully translate the technical and arcane aspects of the story into everyday language, they become sought-out commentators on breaking stories. When teachers strike or threaten to strike, when the school board is cutting programs to balance its budget, when local school councils are being elected or are selecting principals, or when the state's report on test scores for every school is released, the media need help explaining these events. In some venues, such as "the week in review" programs and weekend commentary shows common on TV and radio in the United States, knowledgeable newspeople can provide their own insights. But in most cases, they depend on policy analysts to lend their expertise and outside authenticity to their coverage. This provides a wonderful opportunity for policy-relevant researchers to share their knowledge of the issues more broadly and to help frame the questions raised about the issues.

Different media have different venues for such analysis. The electronic media frequently devote longer conversational formats to explore different dimensions of important stories. On such programs, a policy researcher is able to discuss the application of relevant research (including his/her own), to the problems at hand. On the commercial outlets, these shows are frequently taped toward the end of the week and then aired on Sunday morning or at odd hours such as 1 a.m. Yet it is remarkable how many people are reached by such programs, even during these low-audience slots. On public broadcast stations, these shows may air during weekday mornings or early weeknight evenings. Such shows tend to have smaller audiences than do those on commercial stations, but they are audiences highly attuned to policy issues and frequently include the very policymakers who must act on the issues being discussed. This provides an opportunity for a researcher to make his or her analysis public and targeted to policymakers at the same time. Policymakers then must respond to comments and questions from others who heard the analysis.

The print media frequently carry longer analytical articles in the Sunday newspapers. Sometimes reporters will work on these longer pieces for weeks, and contact a researcher a number of times while developing the full piece. More rarely, a newspaper may develop a series with a number of articles in which a researcher/analyst may be quoted covering a wide range of related issues. For example, in Chicago, the *Tribune* ran a series of articles on the failings of the Chicago schools that stretched over nearly a year and occupied the efforts of four specially assigned reporters for that entire period. The series featured several stories based on themes previously developed by Chicago Panel research reports. The collected articles were eventually published as a book titled *Chicago's Schools: Worst in America?* (*Chicago Tribune,* 1988). With fewer resources, the *Tribune*'s competitor, the *Chicago Sun Times,* featured reform efforts in other major American cities, informing Chicagoans that the proposals being considered in this city had echoes elsewhere. In both cases, there were many opportunities to help the reporters look at issues and developments that policy-relevant researchers thought were important. Sometimes our research was mentioned, and sometimes it was not.

"React" comments to provide balance or depth. One Sunday morning some years ago, my telephone rang. Steve Crocker of Chicago's all-news radio wanted my reaction to the news that the Board of Education and the Chicago Teachers Union had finally reached an agreement on compensation for the year that would prevent a strike halfway through the first semester. Crocker wanted to know what I, as a respected educational researcher and policy analyst, thought about the agreement and what its potential impact would be on the budget and programs of the school system.

Because I have a long relationship with Crocker, I can expect a call from him any morning a school story breaks late the previous day. I can also expect newspaper reporters to call later in the day for a follow-up story, or for a TV news producer to ask if a camera crew can stop by for a brief interview. In all of these situations, no more than one or two sentences and an attribution is likely to appear in the news story. For the reporters, these comments provide either confirmation of what some official has claimed or a contrary view that provides balance. Although most of this kind of coverage is unlikely to advance significantly any policy positions advocated by the analyst, such responses contribute to the analyst's authenticity and provide opportunities for building relationships with the reporters. On some occasions, these "react" interviews can be used to shift the focus of a reporter's story, at which point they can turn into more substantial opportunities.

Deep background. From time to time, policy researchers/analysts find themselves sought out by reporters who wish to conduct in-depth interviews to help provide background and perspective on a story. These conversations may take 2 or 3 hours. Frequent follow-up calls may occur for several weeks as the reporter's project develops. Sometimes, these conversations are an educational experience for a reporter who is new to the policy arena or who is examining an arena he or she expects will become important news later in the year. At other times, a reporter may be working on a specialty story tied to a particular upcoming event, or a reporter may be assigned to do a major story on an issue that the particular media outlet has made a continuing concern. A reporter who has been invited to participate in a week-in-review television show may be seeking clarification of some obscure details of a story he or she has not carefully covered, but expects will arise during the program. The general understanding is that if the researcher/analyst spends a considerable amount of time providing information, he or she will be quoted at several different points in the story as a way of giving credit to the story's source.

Nurturing Contacts With the Press

Researchers looking for occasional exposure in the popular press are fighting an uphill battle. Their research must be particularly relevant to a public policy issue that has high visibility or interest when their report is to be released. Coverage of policy-relevant research is much easier when the researcher/analyst has a long relationship with the members of the press. I am now working with the fourth and fifth generation of education beat reporters at the two major daily newspapers in Chicago. I am one of the "experts" to whom the city editor directs her new education beat reporters for confirmation of their stories. But the relationships with the press must be nurtured. Nurturing requires that researchers

- Use a hook that will interest the audience the press is trying to reach
- Know what kind of story the media are trying to develop
- Focus their information directly on the topic the media are covering
- Keep their comments brief and to the point
- Respond immediately to requests for information
- Give positive feedback to press people when the story is completed

A crucial element in working with the press is to understand their needs. The primary interest of the media is to attract an audience. This is true even for nonprofit public broadcasting companies. Thus, an intelligent researcher seeking coverage should first ask what the potential audience is for the study he or she wants to release; then he or she must consider how to capture that audience. In media jargon, this is called looking for the news hook. What aspect, or angle, of the relevant research will hook the audience into the story? Providing that hook up front, whether in the first announcement of an impending news conference or the first few words of a **sound bite**, makes a reporter's job much easier. The hook has to be authentic, and it has to help sell the reporter's story to his or her editor, who makes the final decision about whether or not to use the story. If the hook works, it will encourage the reporter to come back to the researcher in the future. If the researcher's comments are vague, unfocused, or full of conditional sentences, the reporter's job is harder, and he or she is more likely to seek out someone else for his or her next story. Reporters appreciate sources who make their work easier and who reduce the risk of their making a major error in their reporting.

Definition: A sound bite is a brief statement that powerfully encapsulates the main idea of the interview

It also is important to know the particular needs of the media outlet with which you are working. If you are working with a television reporter, it is important to know the nature of the story he or she is trying to develop and what your role in the story might be. Interviews that do not fit the story that a reporter is trying to develop are a waste of everyone's time. When you know your role in the story, you can find out what the reporter expects you to say about the issue. Frequently, these issues are negotiated with the producer before the interview is scheduled. If your views do not fit the story being developed, you should decline the interview. But if you are happy with the direction of the story and want to contribute to it, then your job is to punch home your point with a few well-chosen words. In all likelihood, the reporter will ask variations of the same question to give you several angles on the point he or she wants made. At times, the interview may be quite lengthy as the reporter tries to think through the story while he or she is gathering information, using you as a resource to help develop the story. You probably will get only about 30 seconds of exposure, but by being helpful, you have made future interviews much more likely.

As with most efforts, the development of trust between a reporter and a policy analyst takes time and nurturing on both sides. But sometimes, a reporter who contacts you is not capable of understanding the intricacies of particular policy issues. In these cases, there is little you can do but correct any mistakes made through letters to the editor and hope that the reporter will move on to another city or a different assignment.

If the media event is a panel discussion on radio or TV, one has to be quick, cogent, and mentally agile. Although these formats allow for longer answers, the researcher must still try to use forceful images and words to punctuate longer descriptions and analyses. You have to be respectful of the other guests, even when strongly disagreeing with them, and deferential to the show's host (who controls whether or not you are invited back). The policy researcher who offends the audience or the host through manner and style is likely to be ignored on the next story.

I learned this lesson the hard way. One evening, I was a guest on one of Chicago's premier news panel shows. After the show, the one woman panelist complained that she had been given few chances to participate. As I walked out of the studio with the host (with whom I thought I had developed a close, respectful relationship over more than 5 years of frequent appearances), I told him that he usually did give men more opportunities to participate than he did women. He interpreted my comment to be an accusation, even though it was offered quietly in a hallway with the hope of helping the host reflect on his own, perhaps unconscious, interaction patterns. More than 3 years passed before I was invited to be a guest on his program again. In many ways, radio's needs are similar to those of television, but radio places a higher premium on articulation and frequently requires an even higher level of intensity among the participants. In recent years, **talk radio** has emerged as a powerful force for shaping public opinion. Talk radio is much more flexible than television. Frequently, experts can participate as guests on hour-long talk shows through telephone links to their home or office. But you must be aware of the context of the show, of the other guests with whom you are appearing, and of undisclosed guests who may be waiting to follow your appearance. These are also lessons that I learned the hard way. I once ended a show on what I felt to be a quite satisfactory note, only to find out later that a second set of guests spent the next hour disparaging what I had said and maligning my motives. These events are not entirely within the control of the policy researcher, but researchers can pick and choose on which outlets to appear. Once a researcher has been victimized on a station, he or she may choose not to make a second appearance.

Definition: 
Talk radio is a radio program in which a host and sometimes an expert guest discuss topics with listeners who call in their comments or questions

With the written press, a research analyst has more opportunity to ramble, to create a context for a story that will be written later in the day (unless the reporter starts the call with those magic words, "I'm on deadline, and . . ."). Not infrequently, the analyst who understands both press needs and an issue—particularly if it is a complex one—can virtually write a reporter's story for him or her, particularly if the reporter is new to the beat. On other occasions, an analyst may have a long conversation with reporters about recent events that never appears in print at all but may lead to several stories at a later time. When reporters have developed a good relationship with a policy researcher or analyst, the latter has an opportunity to point out obscure elements that the reporter may have overlooked. The researcher also may be able to point out links to other prominent newsmakers that will make a reporter's story more valuable to his or her editor.

Finally, nurturing the press is like any other set of important relationships. It is important to tell reporters when they have done a nice job. It is also important to point out things that could have been handled in a better way. At times, it is necessary to do that by responding in the press itself, with a letter to the editor (see Figure 2.2). Most times, it is better to do it in a direct communication, off the record. And from time to time, it is important to put commendations on the record, both for the reporter and for the editor. Everybody likes a pat on the back, and most professionals like assistance in doing their job better, particularly when no one else knows about it.

COOPERATING WITH POLICYMAKERS

Cross Reference: See Hess (1993) in the Suggested Resources section at the end of this chapter

One of the primary ways of cooperating with policymakers is to provide public testimony on policy issues being considered by legislative bodies or administrative staffs. In this section, I describe public policy testimony and the credentials needed to provide it.

School coverage

CHICAGO—I want to commend you for the thoughtful coverage (Nov. 15) of the release of school report card data for the suburban areas. While others in the media took the predictably easy route of glorifying the top scoring districts, your willingness to commit a significant amount of space to both applaud good performance and recognize the difficulties faced by schools with few resources and students with great disadvantages is outstanding.

It is, of course, always a pleasure to read Casey Banas' perceptive coverage. The article on the development of state tests and their ultimate usage for statewide accountability gave the reader a historical perspective most would lack. And "Widening funding chasm: $10,000 a pupil vs. $2,000" continues the thoughtful analysis of inequitable school funding that Banas and Pat Reardon have pioneered.

Those of us concerned to correct this unconscionable condition continue to be grateful to the Tribune both for its coverage and its forthright editorial position. To keep all of this side by side with the regular faithful reporting of results for every school across the metropolitan area creates informed readers, which is the mark of a great newspaper.

G. Alfred Hess Jr.
Executive Director
Chicago Panel on
Public School Policy and Finance

Figure 2.2. A letter to the editor praising a journalist's good reporting.

What Is Public Policy Testimony?

Public policy testimony is given before committees of the legislatures or other governing or administrative bodies. Formal descriptions of legislative testimony usually imply that it provides legislators with a basis for determining whether to support or oppose legislation. In my experience, however, legislation is rarely shaped in legislative hearings, although testimony presented at hearings may be the culmination of a lobbying effort that results in a commitment by committee members to act in certain ways relative to the bill under consideration. Legislators may be given a chance to hold a hearing on a proposal they have made simply to demonstrate to the legislative leaders that they can muster significant support. This was the case in the U.S. Congressional hearing on the Educational Performance Bill mentioned at the beginning of this chapter. If legislators cannot attract well-known and qualified experts to testify in favor of their proposals, the proposals will be dropped from consideration.

A legislative body is not a place to report on scholarly research, although testimony may include such information in a report. Only research that is directly related to the political purposes being served is likely to be solicited. Thus, only research that is policy relevant, and relevant to the particular political processes embodied in particular legislative hearings, is likely to be presented.

Undoubtedly, there is much ethnographic research that might be policy relevant. Similarly, there are social science theories and understandings that, if generally held among legislators, might change the kind of legislation that is adopted. But legislative hearings are not the place to make that case. Hearings are the culmination of the effort to create a consensus among legislators, not the start of that effort. If social scientists wish to create a consensus about needed legislative action, they must start by meeting with and convincing a number of key legislators in private sessions.

Qualifications for Testifying

Experience and connections are the primary qualifications for providing good testimony. Providing legislative testimony is a political, not a scholarly, act, regardless of the rigor of the data on which the testimony is based. Therefore, testimony is more credible if it is presented by people experienced in the political process. I have testified before local, state, or federal legislative bodies more than 45 times. Most of that experience was at the local level, built on policy-relevant research that I and my colleagues had conducted at the local level. Invitations to present formal testimony at the state and federal level generally are generated because the researcher has experience presenting testimony at lower levels in the political system.

But how does a researcher get experience testifying if he or she has not had any? One way is to look to the local community. Opportunities to provide testimony at the local level are fairly frequent in the political processes of the United States and in most other democracies. Most citizens are given an opportunity to provide statements on policy decisions to be made by city councils and boards of education. Frequently, these opportunities arise when legislative bodies, boards of education, or other community agencies are adopting their budgets, because that is when most policy-making bodies determine their priorities. To turn such opportunities into expert testimony requires that a researcher have conducted research relevant to the decision being contemplated. Frequently, reporting on such research simply requires attending the public hearing portion of a meeting of the council or board in question and signing up for a chance to speak. As one's research becomes better known, it may be possible to arrange special times (perhaps with more time available) to provide testimony that the legislators or board members will find particularly valuable.

Another qualification for providing state and federal testimony is connection to political actors. I was invited to testify before the U.S. Congress in 1989 partly because I had helped to write the Chicago School Reform Act of 1988, which loosened bureaucratic requirements on schools in exchange for requiring their accountability in improving student learning. The bill being debated in Congress had a similar intent, so such expertise was relevant. However, I was also chosen to testify because I had worked as staff advisor to an Educational Summit organized by Harold Washington, the Mayor of Chicago, prior to passage of the Chicago reform act. Mayor Washington, a Democrat, previously had served on a key committee of the U.S. House of Representatives. His successor, a Republican from Vermont, hoped to win support for his own school reform bill from Democrats from other states, such as Mayor Washington. He did so by calling to testify someone linked to the mayor who could also be expected to provide credible testimony favorable to his proposed legislation.

Such linkages are not just fortunate accidents. Researchers who want to affect policy must work hard to build such political connections. Working on public or semi-public task forces convened by political or community leaders is one way to begin to know and be known by these leaders. Similarly, working with other policy-relevant researchers and interacting with them at conferences and other research venues may turn out to be valuable in later years. For example, many educational researchers had opportunities to interact with Marshall Smith when he was Dean of the School of Education at Stanford University and a key member of the Consortium on Policy Research in Education during the late 1980s and early 1990s. When Dean Smith became undersecretary in the U.S. Department of Education for the new Clinton administration in 1992, these researchers had a prior connection that then became a direct connection to the federal government's policy-making process.

USING THE COURTS

Public policy is frequently created in legislative bodies. However, legislative acts frequently deny the rights of some citizen in favor of others. One way to correct such inequities is for members of the disadvantaged group to bring a suit in the courts to overturn the legislation or change the way the legislation is being enforced by the federal, state, or local government. Frequently, in such suits, the plaintiffs (those bringing the suit) need research to verify that they are being unfairly disadvantaged.

Policy Research and Legal Action

Case Study

In 1991, a group of rural school districts in the midwestern United States successfully challenged the constitutionality of the state of Missouri's school finance system in the state courts. Their case was joined with a more narrow case brought by a group of suburban school districts around Kansas City. The Kansas City and St. Louis Public Schools each joined the suit as interveners on behalf of the plaintiffs. Meanwhile, four wealthy school districts intervened on behalf of the defense because they feared that the Attorney General's office would not vigorously protect their privileged status under the existing state school finance scheme. As the date for the trial approached, the lawyers for the St. Louis Public Schools realized that they had a problem. The St. Louis Public Schools were the 12th-best funded school system in the state, on a per-pupil basis, and they needed someone to explain to the court (i.e., to the judge) why St. Louis was on the side of the poorly funded plaintiffs and how they had used the money that they had received. Another expert in the case, the president of the American

Education Finance Association (AEFA), on whose board of directors I also served, knew of my experience with the budget and performance of the Chicago Public Schools and recommended that I be retained to make the case for the St. Louis school system.

During the summer, I did a rapid investigation into the school system's revenues and expenditures and of changes in achievement by students in the St. Louis schools. I was able to show that the high level of revenues in St. Louis resulted from orders by the federal court in response to a judgment, first against the school system and then against the State of Missouri, that required the racial desegregation of the city's schools and the establishment of compensatory programs to ensure that African American students in St. Louis would be compensated for the harms done by prior de jure racial segregation of the school system. Prior to 1955, Black and White students were required by state law to attend separate schools. I was able to show that the St. Louis schools expended those desegregation and compensatory revenues in ways that provided an enriched educational program for Black students in the city's schools and that modernized the facilities in which those students were enrolled. Most important, I was able to show that student achievement was improving in the city, but that its students still came to the school system with special needs, largely the result of poverty, that required even more special assistance. Thus, the high revenues received by the St. Louis Public Schools were not the result of preferential benefit under the state's school finance scheme but the result of higher property taxes willingly accepted by St. Louis voters and court-mandated desegregation payments from the state. The level of basic support from the state and the special assistance for meeting special needs of poverty-affected students were still inadequate to the task of providing these students with a high-quality education.

But the major underlying question in the case was whether money had any relationship to student achievement. Ed Hanushek (1986, 1989), an expert in school finance and educational effects, presented evidence to the court to argue that "money doesn't matter," as he had in several other state finance cases. Hanushek's testimony was bolstered by similar testimony from two educational researchers from two elite midwestern universities and an expert from the Missouri education department. The plaintiffs countered with testimony from the president of a third midwestern university, from the nation's premier school finance legislative consultant, the president of the American Educational Finance Association, and myself. Each of us showed that, contrary to the contentions of the state witnesses, money *did* matter in the quality of education made available to the state's students.

In his formal opinion, the judge announced that he found the evidence provided by Hanushek and his colleagues to be not credible. He cited specific portions of the testimony of the plaintiffs' experts that he did find compelling, noting specifically the special needs of students raised in poverty that I had highlighted. But what counted most with the judge was the fact that the rich districts had intervened to defend the current finance system, and that they had hired Hanushek and his colleagues. The judge wrote that arguing that money did not make a difference "is directly contrary to the real positions of the Intervener-Defendants [the wealthy school districts that had hired the "experts"] herein for they would have no interest in this litigation nor would they be paying for litigation costs if it were not for the purpose of preserving the larger amount of school funds on a per pupil basis" (*Committee for Educational Opportunity et al. v. State of Missouri et al.*, 1993, pp. 21f, G3f). He then ruled the state school finance system to be unconstitutional because it unfairly benefited these rich districts and denied equitable assistance to poorer school districts.

Linking With Lawyers

Lawyers conduct litigation. Thus, lawyers hire expert witnesses. To become an expert witness, you have to become known to lawyers. Researchers who have been valuable expert witnesses in the past are already known to lawyers, both those for whom they provided testimony and others who have read the case. The difficulty in this arrangement is that most expert witnesses have been expert witnesses in many cases. This means that their testimony in prior cases is well known both to the lawyers seeking an expert and to the opponents in the case. Such experts need not prove their expertise in court; they simply demonstrate that they have been admitted as experts in numerous other courts. Their prior experience serves as sufficient credentials. But how does an ethnographer become an "expert" in the legal sense for the first time?

Most experts are hired for the first time because they have demonstrated an arena of expertise required by lawyers for one side of a legal dispute and are recommended to the lawyers by someone they already know. My extensive writing about urban school finance, student achievement, taxes, and educational policy were sufficient to convince the lawyers for the St. Louis Public Schools that I could help to support the case they wanted to make in court, deflect objections from the defendant's lawyers, and convince the judge that I knew enough to be worth listening to in court. But these lawyers would not have known about my potential ability to contribute to their work had I not served on the board of directors of the American Educational Finance Association with one of their previously known experts.

To be accepted as an expert, a researcher must be

- Found worthy of being hired to conduct and present some research on behalf of a party to a court action
- Accepted by the court (and the other side) as someone who knows what he or she is talking about, even if, ultimately, the

court reserves the right to decide whether or not the researcher's testimony is credible

The world of litigation is structured quite differently from the world of academic publishing or of policy advocacy. Lawyers who hire and cross-examine witnesses are seeking support for their side's case, evidence that confirms the claims of their clients, and data that can tear apart the testimony of the opposition's experts—not abstract "truth." They do not care that "real" truth may be contrary to their clients' claims.

Litigation, by its very nature, is contentious. Researchers who are not willing to live with these ground rules or who are uncomfortable submitting their work to rigorous attack by other experts, some of whom may be friends and professional colleagues at conferences and in other contexts, should refrain from using this method of dissemination for their research results. However, if you are willing to put your research to the most arduous test, a court judgment supporting the findings of your research has the potential for more widespread effect than does virtually any other venue except enacting legislation.

Working with lawyers requires you to recognize that your job is to provide your side with evidence that will support the arguments to the court and to defend that evidence from strong attack by the opponents. You may be called upon to launch an attack on the research to be provided by the opposition's experts. If you are successful in gaining the confidence of your legal team, you may also be able to suggest approaches and strategies that they might adopt. It is important to remember that your testimony, in most cases, will be only part of the case being mounted by your lawyers. Thus, it is important to fashion your research to be compatible with that of other experts in the case. Whereas academics are accustomed to citing the work of other experts without always defending the credibility of the cited research, in court, such citations are themselves subject to attack. In the St. Louis desegregation case, I did not use research by demographers on population trends in the city of St. Louis to prove that many current students in the St. Louis Public Schools are the children of former students who received an inferior education because of prior racial segregation. Such an argument could show that prior racial segregation affected current student performance because parents were less able to help their children. However, I did work with a demographer from the University of Missouri at St. Louis, who presented the needed demographic data to the court in his own report. His expert testimony documented the changes and similarity in the population over several decades; my testimony drew the educational conclusion about the effects of prior segregation. I would not qualify as an expert on demographics, but I was admitted as an expert on educational policy as it applied to segregation and its effects. Successful support of the case required coordination of research to ensure that the demographer and I, together, could present evidence that would be convincing to the court.

Designing and Conducting Research to Support Expert Testimony

Expert testimony is built upon specific research commissioned or contracted for the case in question and designed to demonstrate a particular conclusion. It may also then involve expressing an opinion about other research presented to the court (notably that provided by the opposition's experts). The contracted research is not an abstract exercise in search of the truth but a focused attempt to build up evidence in support of the legal theory that is the basis of your lawyers' advocacy for their clients' interests. *Thus, a crucial step in providing successful expert testimony is understanding what the legal theory underpinning the case*

Key point

is and what evidence is required to support that theory before the judge. In some cases, an expert who has won the confidence of the legal team may be able to help shape the legal theory.

In the Missouri school finance case, the lawyers for the state argued that money did not make a difference in the achievement of students. Therefore, the state was not perpetrating an injustice upon underfunded school children by allowing local school districts to determine both how much to tax their taxpayers and what level of educational services were appropriate for their children. In opposition, the plaintiffs were seeking to prove that the state had a responsibility to ensure the "general dispersion of knowledge" (a Jeffersonian concept incorporated in the Missouri state constitution[7]), and that an inequitable distribution of funding resulted in an inequitable dispersion of knowledge. In short, the plaintiffs argued that money *does* make a difference. My research, then, was designed to show that the St. Louis Public Schools had used their additional resources in a way to improve the general dispersion of knowledge among the children of the city. The tricky part was to show that the city schools had used the funds effectively, but that there was a still greater need to be met. Fortunately, the data, once carefully assembled, lent themselves to just that conclusion.

Key point

The key, then, was to design a research strategy that was based on a reasonable argument whose main points could be presented clearly to the court. I had to convince my own team that what I proposed was reasonable; that it would be convincing to the judge; that it could withstand the attack of the other side; that it was worth the time, effort, and resources required to produce the needed data; and that it would not produce potentially more damaging data for the other side, which would have access to all of the relevant data through the legal channel of "discovery." This process requires discussions with the lawyers, discussions with the clients who may be expected to produce the required data, discussions with collaborators and assistants, presentation of a proposal to the legal team, and more discussions leading to a decision to go ahead with the planned research project.

Once the research project is approved, the data must be assembled. For an independent policy analyst who is accustomed to cajoling cooperation or is limited to publicly available information, working for the lawyers of a client with a significant interest in the outcome of the legal action can mean a wonderful change in ease of access to information. In the St. Louis case, failure to win the court case could mean the loss of millions of dollars to the district and result in cutting many jobs in the bureaucracy. Policy analysts find that busy bureaucrats who are ordinarily unreachable suddenly leap to return calls, because the court case takes priority over normal operations. Prior commitments are set aside to accommodate the analysts' travel schedule. Intrusiveness and inconvenience are expected by the lawyers and willingly accommodated by the clients, although the sensitive researcher will try to mitigate such impact as much as possible.

On the other hand, getting information from the other side is much more difficult. The typical way to secure information from the opposition is to file a series of data requests with the court. If the court agrees that the requests are appropriate, it will require the opposition to answer. The opposition has the right to protest supplying this information, and the court must be persuaded that your need for the information is appropriate to the case and will not cause the opposition irreparable harm in other matters not before the court. Interrogatories and public reports are the primary vehicles for receiving information about the opponents. A supplementary vehicle is the evidence contained in reports that the opposition and their experts provide to the court. Lawyers on your side and their clients have a right to receive all of the data upon which these reports are based. Thus, you can request the same database provided by the opponents to their own experts. Conversely, they have a right to the data you generate for your research.

Requests for information from the other side are contested at every turn by their lawyers. Each piece of requested information must be carefully specified and justified to the court by your lawyers. And you have to be very careful to ask for everything you need, because you will certainly be provided nothing more than you request. Follow-up requests are likely to be delayed, ignored, postponed until the information is no longer useable, or actively protested before the court as an unwarranted intrusion into the ongoing operations of the opposition's clients. The data themselves may be trivial, but the request gives the opposition's lawyers an opportunity to impugn your expertise before you ever get to submit a report to the court. This factor may make your own lawyers unwilling to request data. To summarize: Litigation is a highly complex judicial dance choreographed in a manner totally unfamiliar to the first-time expert!

Our opponents in St. Louis were entitled to acquire data that we developed. That fact convinced lawyers in the St. Louis desegregation case not to implement the part of my proposed research design that called for surveying parents of St. Louis public school children about their own educational backgrounds. Our lawyers worried that developing that data would, at the same time, provide evidence for the opposition's experts, who were expected to argue that any lowered achievement levels of St. Louis students was caused by lower parental capacity, rather than (our argument) by inadequacies in the St. Louis school system that resulted from prior segregation and that could be overcome by additional state funding for desegregation efforts. Thus, our lawyers made a judgment call that the potential for benefit by our opponents from our collecting these data was higher than the potential benefit to our own case.

To compensate for the absence of these direct data, we developed an alternative strategy that used the demographic studies mentioned above to demonstrate indirectly the continuity between prior students negatively affected by segregation (a judgment already made in earlier opinions of the court) and their children now attending the St. Louis Public Schools. ***Thus, research designs must accommodate not only the most direct and effective approaches to proving a point but also the potentially disadvantageous uses of the data to be collected.*** This is a complexity not normally encountered in academic or policy advocacy research.

Key point

Once the data are collected and analyzed, they must be marshaled into a powerful and persuasive argument for presentation to the court. The strategy is to support your client's case as strongly as you can while hiding weaknesses that might serve to support your opponents' interests. This is not dispassionate research. This is oppositional research designed to win a conflict.

The data presented to the court usually take one of two formats. The first is quite lengthy, with powerful contributing evidence. The second is quite sketchy, designed simply to qualify the expert for inclusion in the case. Regardless of their format, such reports are designed to state the researcher's case as powerfully as possible. Thus, instead of anticipating criticism by stating all of the caveats about weaknesses in your approach or data at the beginning of the report, expert testimony is designed to make the strongest possible assertions while hiding, as well as possible, the weaknesses of the argument. Because many of these arguments have been presented previously in courts in other jurisdictions, it is not infrequent that expert testimony also contains a fair number of preemptive attacks against the opposition's experts in anticipation of their attempts to rebut your testimony. The researcher who is not prepared for such contestation should not engage in expert testimony.

Exchanging Information

As indicated previously, the basic process for providing expert testimony in litigation is to do a piece of specific research designed to support the arguments of your lawyers. This research is written up in the form of a report to the court. In preparation for the trial, the judge will establish a calendar, including dates by which each side must list the experts it intends to use as part of its case and when the expert reports are due to the court. Usually, the report is due 2 to 3 months prior to the beginning of the trial. The expert's reports are then submitted to all parties in the case. Sometimes, if circumstances are not related to tardiness on the part of the researcher, the court will allow a later submission of an expert's report, as was granted for my report in the Missouri school finance case.

At this point, an expert witness may also be asked by his or her side's lawyers to review the reports of one or more of the opposition experts. In that event, your job is to review the opposition's report to determine whether the evidence presented is damaging to the case your lawyers are trying to build. Presumably, unless the opposition has wasted its money, it will be. Your review, then, is to determine the strengths and weaknesses of the opposition's report. Your lawyers need to know where the strengths of the report are so that they are prepared for the report's most damaging effect on their case. You can be most helpful if you can identify the weaknesses of the report and suggest alternative responses or simple-to-perform research that can mitigate the effects of the opposition's report. A good expert witness will have crafted his or her report to hide these weaknesses as much as possible. Your job is to identify them for your lawyers so that, on cross-examination, the opposition expert will be put on the defensive trying to preserve the strengths of his or her report while its weaknesses are exposed to the court. In some cases, the weaknesses may be so huge that the opposition's whole report can be discounted.

Your lawyers have two strategies available to them relative to an opposition's expert report. On one hand, they may simply prepare for a withering cross-examination, seeking to undermine the credibility of the report with the judge. If the opposition report is not seen to be very damaging, or if the expert is known to be easily rattled when presenting and defending his or her testimony, this may be the preferred strategy. It has the clear advantage of conserving the client's resources by not paying for further research designed to disprove the opposition's findings.

A second strategy is to solicit formal responses to an opposition report that undermine the opposition's credibility even before the trial begins. These responses can be filed with the court. This was done in the St. Louis desegregation case. The state hired David Armor, an expert often used by state and city boards of education trying to defend themselves against charges of perpetuating or permitting segregation. Armor's job was to show that the actions of the St. Louis Public Schools had eliminated the "vestiges of segregation,"[8] with the massive help of state resources, such that any remaining differences in student achievement were simply the effects of poverty. Unfortunately for him, a careful reading of his report indicated that he had included in his regression analyses an incorrect number for the proportion of African Americans in St. Louis living in poverty. His formula indicated that 98% of all African Americans in St. Louis lived below the poverty line. He further compounded the problem by using census data for all St. Louis white families to calculate the poverty levels of white students in the public schools, even though 60% of white students did not attend the public schools. When Professor Bill Trent (University of Illinois) and I pointed out these problems in rebuttal reports filed with the court, Armor was forced to admit his mistake, run a whole new set of calculations, and drastically reduce the proportion of achievement difference he claimed could be ascribed simply to poverty. By contrast, my report was designed to argue that even the poverty level of current African American students was a continuing "vestige" of the prior segregated education received by their parents. Thus, even before getting to trial, the quality of Armor's workmanship had been seriously challenged, and he had been forced to admit his mistake, which weakened his claim to credibility.

Unfortunately, while you are busy challenging the work of the opposition's experts, your own work is receiving similar scrutiny by the opposition. Their experts also may file rebuttal briefs, which then requires filing a response brief if their rebuttal seriously damages your findings. If their rebuttal does not seriously damage your testimony, again the cheapest response may be no response.

The opposition has a further opportunity to probe the weaknesses in your potential testimony by taking a deposition from you about your proposed testimony prior to the trial. Being deposed is similar to a long, tiring cross-examination in which the opposition lawyers try to poke holes in the credibility of your background and expertise or the research you intend to present to the court. In a deposition, the expert witness is under oath, and a court reporter records everything that is said. A printed, verbatim account of the deposition is presented to you for review for accuracy. The corrected account of the deposition is filed with the court and can be introduced into the trial. The deposition allows the opposition to fully probe every aspect of your testimony without tying up the court in lengthy proceedings.

Academics and policy advocates must remember that their job in a deposition is not to convince opposition lawyers of the correctness of their research (their job is to be unconvinced) but to provide them with as few opportunities to attack the testimony as possible. Although the propensity of most researchers is to expound on their findings and to show all the little "ins and outs" of what they did, doing this while being deposed gives the opposition tools with which to attack their research in court. Thus, expert witnesses are most effective when they can limit themselves to answering the questions asked by the opposition lawyer as briefly but as straightforwardly as possible.

Giving Testimony

Finally, your lawyers have put together their case. The trial begins, and you, the expert, are called to testify. In all likelihood, the court has given them specific limitations on how they can present their case. In the St. Louis desegregation case, the school board's lawyers were allocated 20 hours for their case, including both presentation of their own witnesses and cross-examination of witnesses presented by other parties to the case. In this case, there were two different plaintiff groups that had brought the original lawsuit in the 1970s against the city schools; the St. Louis Board of Education; the state (whom the city board had successfully sued after losing the original case); the suburban school districts that had been cajoled by the court into a cooperative, interdistrict transfer program;[9] and the U.S. Department of Justice, which had intervened in the original case on behalf of the plaintiffs. Thus, the city board's lawyers had to decide how much time they wanted to spend presenting testimony from each of their own experts and how much time they wanted to save to attack the testimony of experts from the other parties. With our expert reports already filed and on record with the court, and thus able to be incorporated in the final arguments on the case, our lawyers decided to present only a bare-bones summary of the report as direct testimony, a process that took only half an hour. In that way, the opposition had to use its time in cross-examination, during which I could continue to make points from my report, and the school board's lawyers could save their time for cross-examination of Armor and the state's other witnesses.

By contrast, in the school finance lawsuit, the St. Louis board's lawyers recognized that the judge was looking for ways to decide the case in favor of the plaintiffs. During the pretrial motions and in the first few days of the case, it became obvious that the judge was convinced by the evidence already filed with the court that the state's system was unconstitutional. He was simply looking for the arguments that could bolster his final opinion and judgment, making it more difficult for higher courts to reverse his decision should the case be appealed. Therefore, the city schools' lawyers, in this case in an ancillary role as interveners rather than as the primary plaintiffs, wanted my testimony presented as fully as possible. My direct testimony took more than 2 hours, and the cross-examination required 2 more days, providing an unexpected opportunity. As the judge adjourned court for the day, he stepped down from the bench and walked me to the rail of the unused jury box and engaged me in a half-hour conversation about possible courses he could take! In this informal setting, he could probe my thinking about strengths and weaknesses of potential solutions without the fractiousness of cross-examination and objections. And best of all, this was free time, not chargeable to our side's presentation time.

Unfortunately, before an analyst you can even present testimony, he or she must be accepted by the court as a qualified expert. The easiest solution for the opposition is to get the court to dismiss an analyst's work because he or she is not recognized as an expert in the area the report covers. As previously noted, the easiest way to achieve expert status is to cite acceptance as an expert by other courts. But how does anyone become an expert the first time? In the second Missouri trial, the state's lawyers tried to disqualify me because I had never previously presented testimony in a desegregation case. The city's lawyers countered that I had studied desegregation in Chicago, had written extensively about desegregation (Hess, 1984; Hess & Warden, 1988), and had studied the St. Louis Public Schools previously in the Missouri school finance case. With the understanding that he could review his decision after hearing my testimony, the judge accepted me as an expert.

Presenting testimony is not the same as reading a report to the judge or even presenting a summary of the report, as one might at a professional conference. Lawyers decide the main points they want you to emphasize. They will then structure a set of questions that will elicit from you your background, your expertise, what they asked you to do, what you did, and the opinions you formed as a result of your research (i.e., your findings). Your job as the expert is to answer their questions as fully as possible, referring to data in your report as appropriate, but not jumping ahead to the next point until asked. From time to time, you may be interrupted by a question of clarity from the judge or by an objection from the opposition lawyer. Objections can be particularly frustrating times, because unless you are asked to comment by the judge, the lawyers will argue about what you are saying as if you were not present. You can have no role in the debate, even though it directly affects you and your work.

When your lawyers are satisfied that they have presented to the court the parts of the report needed for their concluding argument, the opposition lawyers have the opportunity to cross-examine you. Their decisions are shaped by their time limits. They must decide how important it is to their case to undermine your testimony. If you are attacking the central lines of their argument, as my report in the desegregation case did, they may choose to spend several hours attempting either to poke holes in your argument or to discredit your work. Your job is to defend the appropriateness of your findings, based on the evidence you have gathered and presented to the court. Again, this becomes a battle of wits. The opposition lawyers will try to confuse you; get you to say something that contradicts something else you have said; or show that elsewhere you may have written something, even years previously, that contradicts what you have presented in court. Your job is to carefully show the court the differences in circumstances that lead to different conclusions in different cases, or to justify why you have changed your mind about something over a period of time, if you have. During cross-examination, you are mostly on the defensive, but at times, the opposition provides openings for you to make points that would not be sustainable on the basis of the research you conducted for the case. These opportunities to attack the basic unfairness of the current situation can be powerful with the court. It was just such repartee under cross-examination immediately prior to the day's adjournment that led to the informal conversation with the judge in the school finance suit.

Awaiting the Judgment

Unfortunately, unlike in a fictional courtroom drama, judicial decisions are rarely announced at the conclusion of the trial. The judge, in a major public policy case, is likely to take several months before issuing his or her judgment and opinion. Frequently, the judge will ask the lawyers for the side he or she favors to submit a draft opinion and draft orders they would wish him or her to enter.

In all likelihood, experts will not even be present for the conclusion of the trial unless it happens that they testify on the last day of the trial. The school finance trial took 2 full weeks to present. The desegregation case took 3 weeks. Expert witnesses are paid only for the time they are actually doing the research, presenting it in court, or waiting to be called to testify. Most expert witnesses do not wait around in court for the judgment to be announced.

The court's first decision is which side's experts it believes. Because court decisions in the United States are formally recorded and may become the basis for further court decisions, having testimony favorably commented upon and findings cited becomes an important vehicle for disseminating research. More important, through the orders entered by the court, research can have direct, practical impact on behalf of the clients for whom a researcher has been employed. Thus, a favorable judgment can be very satisfying.

CONCLUSION

There are a number of different ways in which policy-relevant research can be used to change, or preserve, current social patterns. It can be used to

- Change the way the public thinks about social problems
- Create opportunities for new policies to be established
- Insert policy researchers directly into the policy-setting process through formal testimony before groups of policymakers
- Allow researchers to participate in formal litigation where courts dictate how policies should be implemented and how the rights of citizens are to be protected

These means of disseminating research are very different from traditional academic venues such as journal articles, published books, and papers presented at professional conferences. More important, they are vehicles for research dissemination that promise immediate impact.

Qualitative research can be an important contributor to such efforts. The strength of qualitative research is that it is focused on particular social realities, and rather than simply providing a statistical measure of inequity, it can make evident the inequities experienced by real people. It can answer the questions, "How was this policy implemented?

Why did it work the way it did? How did people react to the policy? Were there unforeseen consequences or problems that were not expected?" When combined with quantitative data that, for example, enumerates how many people were affected, or how many schools really changed, or how much achievement scores changed, policy-relevant research can be important in deciding which policies to change and which to maintain—even though the vehicles for disseminating such research are quite different from those for more typical academic research.

NOTES

1. "Trashing" is a colloquialism, meaning "to speaking negatively about something in an unfair fashion."

2. This research strategy echoed the earlier work of researchers at Michigan State University (Brookover & Lezotte, 1979; Edmonds, 1979) who identified the distinguishing characteristics of "effective" inner-city elementary schools.

3. For example, we knew that Black students and Hispanic students had higher dropout rates than white students and that lower-income students dropped out more frequently than did more affluent students. A regression analysis allowed us to show that it was the income level of the student that was more important than the race of the student in understanding which students dropped out more frequently.

4. Outliers are schools whose dropout rates were significantly above or below a line drawn on a graph to represent the increasing average dropout rate for schools as the percentage of their entering students reading below grade level increased.

5. Readers should also keep in mind that public policies are guided by social ethics, and that individual stakeholders may have their own "theories" of how things work and why they are the way they are. Thus the role of theory in policy research is both important and not always straightforward.

6. The following section is adapted from an article (Hess, 1992) that originally appeared as "Popular Coverage of Policy Relevant Research," in *Practicing Anthropology, 14*(4), 27-31.

7. Thomas Jefferson, one of the founding fathers of the United States of America, provided much of the philosophical underpinnings of governance for the new country. His ideas about education were incorporated into the constitutions of many of the country's states.

8. Elimination of all "vestiges" (lingering effects) of segregation was a goal of the original 1980 judgment against the St. Louis Public Schools.

9. Each day, some 12,000 St. Louis students were bussed to schools in 26 surrounding communities; about 1,000 suburban students were bussed to city magnet schools.

REFERENCES

Brookover, W. B., & Lezotte, L. W. (1979). *Changes in school characteristics coincident with changes in student achievement.* East Lansing: Michigan State University Press.

Bryk, A. S., Easton, J. Q., Kerbow, D., Rollow, S. G., & Sebring, P. A. (1993). *A view from the elementary schools: The state of reform in Chicago.* Chicago: Consortium on Chicago School Research.

Chicago Tribune. (1988). *Chicago's schools: Worst in America?* Chicago: Author.

Designs for Change. (1985). *The bottom line: Chicago's failing schools and how to save them.* Chicago: Author.

Easton, J. Q., Bryk, A. S., Driscoll, M. E., Kotsakis, J. G., Sebring, P. A., & van der Ploeg, A. J. (1991). *Charting reform: The teachers' turn.* Chicago: Consortium on Chicago School Research.

Edmonds, R. (1979, October). Effective schools for the urban poor. *Educational Leadership, 37,* 15-18.

Hanushek, E. A. (1986). The economics of schooling: Production and efficiency in public schools. *Journal of Economics Literature, 24,* 1141-1177.

Hanushek, E. A. (1989). The impact of differential expenditures on school performance. *Educational Researcher, 18*(4), 45-51.

Hess, G. A., Jr. (1984). Renegotiating a multicultural society: Participation in desegregation planning in Chicago. *Journal of Negro Education, 53,* 132-146.

Hess, G. A., Jr. (1992). Popular coverage of policy-relevant research. *Practicing Anthropology, 14*(4), 27-31.

Hess, G. A., Jr. (1993). Testifying on the Hill: Using ethnographic data to shape public policy. In D. M. Fetterman (Ed.), *Speaking the language of power: Communication, collaboration and advocacy* (pp. 38-49). Washington, DC: Falmer.

Hess, G. A., Jr. (1995). *Restructuring urban schools: A Chicago perspective.* New York: Teachers College Press.

Hess, G. A., Jr. (Ed.). (1996). *Implementing reform: Stories of stability and change in 14 schools.* Chicago: Chicago Panel on School Policy.

Hess, G. A., Jr., & Lauber, D. (1985). *Dropouts from the Chicago public schools.* Chicago: Chicago Panel on Public School Finances.

Hess, G. A., Jr., & Warden, C. A. (1988). Who benefits from desegregation now? *Journal of Negro Education, 57,* 536-551.

Hess, G. A., Jr., Wells, E., Prindle, C., Kaplan, B., & Liffman, P. (1986). *"Where's Room 185?" How schools can reduce their dropout problem.* Chicago: Chicago Panel on Public School Policy and Finance.

Ryan, W. (1976). *Blaming the victim.* New York: Random House.

SUGGESTED RESOURCES

Hess, G. A., Jr. (1993). Testifying on the Hill: Using ethnographic data to shape public policy. In D. M. Fetterman (Ed.), *Speaking the language of power: Communication, collaboration and advocacy* (pp. 38-49). Washington, DC: Falmer.

Hess, G. A., Jr. (1995). *Restructuring urban schools: A Chicago perspective.* New York: Teachers' College Press.

Hess, G. A., Jr. (Ed.). (1996). *Implementing reform: Stories of stability & change in 14 schools.* Chicago: Chicago Panel on School Policy.

Hess, G. A., Jr., Wells, E., Prindle, C., Kaplan, B., & Liffman, P. (1986). *"Where's Room 185?" How schools can reduce their dropout problem.* Chicago: Chicago Panel on Public School Policy and Finance.

3

USING ETHNOGRAPHY TO ENHANCE PUBLIC PROGRAMMING

Lynne Williamson
Jeremy Brecher
Ruth Glasser
Jean J. Schensul

INTRODUCTION

This chapter provides a set of procedures and case examples to guide the development and implementation of public programming based on ethnographic field research. Our emphasis is on the ways in which ethnographic data (observations, recorded and videotaped in-depth interviews and oral histories) are transformed into public programs of interest to a broad audience. We believe that this transformation can occur most effectively when set in the context of strong collaborative working relationships with community scholars and traditional artists. The term

AUTHORS' NOTE: All authors have contributed to the section of the chapter titled "Collaboration in Public Ethnography and Public Programming." The case studies in the chapter show readers how the principles described in the introduction are incorporated into actual examples of public programming based on community ethnography. They represent the fieldwork and public programs conducted by each author, and for this reason, they are separately authored. Jean J. Schensul, Series Coeditor, integrated and edited the chapter for Book 7 and also added methods sections.

Definition: A public program is an activity that represents to the public the culture and art forms of one or more communities using a variety of media, including radio, film, gallery exhibits, and performances

public programs refers to radio and television broadcasts, films, performances, gallery exhibitions, books, and other public events that present or portray cultures through their histories and material and artistic expressions to a diversity of audiences. Commitment to authenticity of cultural representation and inclusion of members of the communities themselves as partners in the process of research and program development should be central characteristics of public programming based on ethnographic research.

The four authors who have contributed to the chapter have worked together and separately on public programming. The strength of their work lies in the commonality of their views on the relationship between research, communities, and public programs, combined with somewhat different disciplinary affiliations and program directions. Jeremy Brecher is a community historian who is well known for his text on developing history from the people's perspective (Brecher, 1996), as well as for several widely recognized publications on the labor movement including *Building Bridges: The Emerging Grassroots Coalition of Labor and Community* (Brecher & Costello, 1990). In this chapter, he describes the process of producing a collaborative written and filmed history of brass workers in the Naugatuck Valley of Connecticut based on **participatory oral history.**

Definition: Participatory oral history refers to involving people in the writing of their own histories, collected and interpreted through their reports of their own experience

Ruth Glasser is a historian with a community organizing background. She joined Jeremy Brecher as one member of a team committed to developing a series of radio programs and ethnic music festivals in Waterbury, Connecticut as an outgrowth of community history. She has remained involved in both the production of educational materials on the music and culture of ethnic groups in the area, and the production of scholarly works on Puerto Rican history and musical traditions (Glasser, 1995) and migration (Glasser, 1997). She reflects on the reciprocal relationship between public programming and scholarly literature.

Lynne Williamson directs the Connecticut Cultural Heritage Arts Program at the Institute for Community Research. With a scholarly background in anthropology, folklore, and museum work, she has engaged the program with approximately 135 artists and more than 50 distinct ethnic/national groups in Connecticut. Working together with representatives of many of these groups and with academic scholars, she has developed and produced visual and performance projects through the Institute for Community Research community arts gallery and elsewhere in the state (Williamson, 1994, 1995, 1996, 1997). She integrates representative art forms and the perspectives of academically based and community scholars to convey a comprehensive picture of a group's history and culture through its heritage arts.

Jean J. Schensul, Director of the Institute for Community Research[1] since 1987, initiated the Connecticut Cultural Heritage Arts program at the Institute with the assistance of David Marshall, an arts administrator and anthropologist at the Connecticut Commission on the Arts, and with the encouragement and financial support of the Folk Arts Program of the National Endowment for the Arts.[2] She has been active at the interface of community arts, education, prevention, and public programs since the mid-1980s (Schensul, 1990).

Each of these authors contributes a unique perspective on the relationship between ethnography and public programming. The chapter consists of two major sections: an introduction to the principles of using ethnography in public programming, and three case examples exemplifying these principles and methods at work. The primary methodological and philosophical issues are discussed in the first section. Additional important methodological points and suggestions emerge in the case examples in the second part of the chapter. Each case example and the chapter as a whole concludes with checklists of important considerations in developing public programs based on collaborative ethnographic research.

COLLABORATION IN PUBLIC ETHNOGRAPHY AND PUBLIC PROGRAMMING

All too often, both research projects and programming arising out of the research are conducted by specialists for other specialists. Such projects have a top-down approach, whereby scholars impose their sense of how to conduct research and how to use its results. When the field of inquiry—such as anthropology, folklore, sociology, or ethnohistory—relates to the cultures or practices of other societies, the top-down approach is neither sufficient for good research nor respectful to the people studied. Likewise, when public or educational programming is constructed using this approach, the results can be alienating to the people whose cultures are presented and are often inaccurate as representations of these cultures.

After many years of engaging in cultural expressions within their own communities, such as socials, festivals, traditional arts productions, storytelling, or family gatherings, community groups are influencing the way more public cultural programming is done throughout the United States. Often, out of a sense of frustration at the way they have been misrepresented in public programs as well as in research, Native Americans and many other ethnic groups based in America are developing their own projects to present their cultures to public audiences. Tourism and economic development sometimes are important components of community projects. However, the key goals of these groups are more likely to be public education, authenticity of presentation, and service to the community.

The upsurge in community-driven cultural presentations has been powered by several forces. Members of some ethnic groups are eager to bring to public attention activities that have been happening naturally within their communities for a long time. A major reason cited by community groups for wanting to produce their own projects is the desire to retain control over the way their cultures are presented. They are not willing to make their own models and methods of interpretation fit expected institutional requirements or existing norms. Another objective important to these groups is to give audiences a real (as opposed to virtual or theatrical) experience, a chance for the public to meet members of the culture in a more natural, informal, and actual life setting.

It is helpful to keep in mind that neither ethnographers nor community culture bearers necessarily know the entire history of their community or the cultural/art forms to be represented in public programming. Ethnographic research can enhance the authenticity of public programming by using narrative forms to reveal the community's history with the art form, the art form's meaning, and the diversity of opinion in the community about it. The examples cited here are intended to illustrate the strengths inherent in a collaborative approach to public programming, as well as the richer cultural understandings that arise from direct contact with members of communities or ethnic groups who encourage others to experience their cultures through participation and education.

Ethnographers involved in research for public programming will find it especially beneficial to collaborate with those groups that have a clear commitment and desire to present their cultural experiences to the public. In such cases, the exchange of research and technical presentation skills that ethnographers can offer or facilitate blends well with a group's vision of how it wishes to present itself. The joint investigation that occurs enhances the quality of the programming and, at the same time, enriches the quality of the research.

This chapter discusses the development of public programming based on ethnographic research conducted collaboratively with a variety of communities. The authors have participated in public programs, including art and history exhibits, radio and television features, books, articles, catalogues and brochures, festivals and concerts, tours, teacher training workshops, lectures and discussions, and cultural performances in schools. Their experiences are used to describe ways of developing solid educational and entertaining public programs in partnership with communities and their members, starting with some guidelines recommended for those contemplating a public programming project.

Guiding Principles

It is important to outline some of the concepts and conflicts that underlie public ethnography projects and that have proven enlightening in seeking to improve these projects. Some readers may find the ideas provocative. None of these insights has been attained easily. Most were learned the hard way through months and years of hands-on experience.

- Knowledge is power.
- "Insiders" and "outsiders," working together, create the richest interpretations.
- People and peoples are not homogeneous.
- Enhancing capacity and understanding for all parties is important overall.
- Community arts aim to conserve while fostering organic creativity.
- Patience is critical for achieving desired outcomes.

Knowledge is power. For full participation and genuine dialogue in a democratic society, information and ideas must be available to the public, not just to groups of specialists. To be accessible, knowledge must be in forms and formats that can be accessed easily and used by a variety of people. Public programming is, fundamentally, a form of information sharing. At its best, it can be developed through a process that is itself a form of power sharing, as those whose cultural practices are being exhibited, discussed, or otherwise represented take on decision-making roles in framing the public presentation of information. Often, those represented through ethnographically informed public programming historically have held limited power. The process of direct involvement in representation enhances their influence, informs the ethnographers, and enriches the program's base of information.

"Insiders" and "outsiders," working together, create the richest representations. Both members and nonmembers of a group can contribute valuable information and expertise to the understanding and presentation of a group's history and culture. Insiders know from birth or long experience the subtleties and deep cultural meanings within a group. Outsiders bring a view derived from their experiences that provides comparison and alternative perspectives. Neither has a monopoly on truth or objectivity. Subtle forms of intellectual arrogance, such as considering one's approach to be wider, more informed, or more educated, dismiss other forms of knowledge. Incorporating a variety of different perspectives enriches an endeavor. In situations where disputes over information, styles, or modes of presentation arise, the outcomes need to be carefully negotiated with respect to differences. Sometimes, different views can be placed side by side and given equal weight, such as in a text or exhibit label. Seeking to present a unified, coherent approach or picture can mislead, stereotype, or gloss over important differences.

People and peoples are not homogeneous. Communities are sometimes characterized by internal differences or conflicts, as well as by their distinctiveness in relation to the world around them. A community is, after all, a collection of individuals. Understanding the political and social dynamics that occur in communities requires attention to both explicit and unvoiced communication from collaborators and colleagues as well as a rigorous self-criticism on the part of the field-workers/program developer. The key is to investigate through research and, at the same time, to intuit what is actually happening in a community, even if no clear pattern or "party line" seems evident.

Enhancing capacity and understanding for all parties is important. The purpose of public programming in partnership with communities goes beyond completion of a project or production of an event. The wider, long-term goal is to enhance capacity and understanding for all parties. The process of working together, of building trust through reciprocity, is as important as the product: the event or program produced. Information should not flow only one way, from informant to researcher. By offering technical assistance, advice, and social support, and by demonstrating a genuine commitment to power sharing through candid discussions and joint decision making, researchers contribute to a process that benefits community partners in tangible ways. In return, these community experts teach researchers and scholars about the underlying, sometimes unwritten realities of their lives and cultures.

Community arts aim to conserve while fostering organic creativity. Community arts aim to preserve cultural practices while also encouraging the organic development or natural outgrowth of new creative expressions based on these traditions. The apparent disjuncture between the "old ways" and innovations can be uncomfortable for those who retain stereotypical images or expectations of a cultural group, and such dissonances can be challenging to present. In such cases, interpretation provides the key as the people whose lives are both represented and affected become involved in offering information from their inside perspective. Many groups are insisting on being full partners in the process of deciding upon and portraying more accurately the full range of variation in cultural expression in their communities.

Patience is critical. It can take years for the full results of a project or aspects of a project to achieve fruition. Often, success can best be measured in small increments that, in their cumulative effect, lead to a powerful conclusion. The work of folklorists often takes the form of delayed gratification, because the essence of this work is to build trust, create networks, spend quality time with individuals and groups, and learn to understand another culture—none of which happens quickly. Some of our deepest relationships with traditional artists, for example, have developed over time as we have met them, learned about their work, provided technical assistance as needed, collaborated on programs, offered advice, enjoyed their successes, and kept in touch. Several of the artists have received their immigration cards under the category "artists of exceptional merit" during the time they were involved with projects described in this chapter; several others have started businesses based on their artwork. The wider recognition these artists gained through participating in different projects and the networks they were able to access through these programs contributed to their successes, even though this sometimes took several years.

Steps to Develop Public Programming Out of Ethnographic Fieldwork

- Plan public programs before the research is conducted.
- Make sure that the public program's philosophy is consistent with that of the overall, longer-term project.
- Be realistic about what can be accomplished with available time and financial resources.
- Build important relationships from the beginning through field research and participant observation. Relationships form the basis for good public programming partnerships.
- Consider whom you want to reach at the beginning.
- Remember that communities incorporate a variety of different groups and attitudes.
- Build a strong interdisciplinary research team with experience in the community to be represented in the program.
- Consider carefully the role of all participants as well as your own. Review roles and responsibilities reflexively on an ongoing basis.
- Be careful about singling out individuals for special attention; this may disrupt community cohesiveness.
- Consider and address conflicting agendas.
- Make sure that program decision making is shared between researchers and community participants.
- Incorporate technical assistance and information exchange into program development so that community participants and researchers can share expertise and learn from one another.
- Request and respond to feedback from the participating community.
- Try a number of small pilot projects over time rather than a single large event held at the end of the project.

Key point

The time to think about public programming as a component of a larger project or research initiative is not when the research is finished but when the entire project is first

conceptualized and developed. The **programs** (i.e., events), as components of a larger **project,** should have the same inspiration, objectives, and design as the project as a whole—that is, using research to enhance capacity, educate, give voice to, and collaborate with communities and individuals.

Definition: A project is a large, longer term effort with a number of different components; a public program is a single public event or performance that is often part of a larger project

It is important to be realistic about what can be accomplished and how long it will take. The competition for grants, media coverage, and public recognition push public programmers to propose complex, multipart projects and to make extravagant promises about what they will do. But promising more than can reasonably be delivered is a certain formula for disappointment. We have all observed or worked on projects that poured massive efforts into the research phase only to run out of time, money, and energy before the public presentations were complete. The initial planning should define the public programs to be developed, as well as provide a realistic time line for implementing all stages, making sure that all materials and work needed receive a high priority throughout the entire project, not just at the end.

Key point 

Relationships should be built from the very beginning. ***Most successful projects are based on effective networking, a process enhanced by meeting and talking on a regular basis to as many people as possible in a community or group.*** One of the ways in which a researcher can both learn about and be accepted into a group is to "hang out," or participate socially by attending community events, frequenting local stores and restaurants, visiting homes informally, and tagging along with family groups (with their prior permission, of course!). This process is referred to as participant observation. The best conversations and stories often begin around the dinner table, after the microphone is turned off and the taped interview questions stop. Whether people want to work with an ethnographer will be greatly affected

Key point 

Cross Reference: See Books 1and 2 for a discussion of participant observation

by whether they perceive the researcher as someone who treats people with respect and seems genuinely interested in their lives. If they do, the relationship builds trust, and the information is more interesting and useful to both parties.

Key point

Think about whom you want to reach. ***Successful public programming must take audience and audience needs into account.*** To involve members of a particular community, it is important to learn how the community organizes and arranges its own community functions, and then attend these. It is also important to learn about the constraints that might keep people from attending. Encouraging working people to participate means scheduling meetings and events at times they can attend. Programs that involve elderly people, or single mothers with young children, need to consider providing transportation. It does not work to devise a wonderful plan or program that by virtue of its structure excludes the very people one hopes to reach.

Key point

No community is homogeneous. All communities incorporate a variety of different groups and attitudes. A researcher/programmer who becomes identified with one sector or faction of a community faces the risk of being shunned or even campaigned against by others. If only one group or individual is accepted as representative of the whole community, others may feel excluded. The ethnographer should seek to understand diversity of expression within the community in order to facilitate accurate representation in public programming. Learning about and coming to understand differences within a cultural group can be part of the educational process that public programming is designed to promote, helping to dispel stereotypical notions of "monolithic" communities.

Key point

Building a project team is essential to developing a good program. A project team may start with the research staff but may expand to include anyone who is interested in the program's topic. It is important to include on your team

community scholars and experts, academic researchers with community experience and others with special expertise related to the program. Community scholars are experts on specific aspects of their own community history and culture, recognized for their depth of knowledge and experience regardless of their level of formal education or training. After years of promotion, this notion is now better understood and accepted by university-based scholars as an authentic viewpoint that is as important as a more academic or literary perspective. It is worth making what may be a special effort to find such people because of the special contributions they can make to the program and the benefits that accrue to the community. The important thing is to pull together a well-defined group whose members are willing to share responsibility for the project and who are fully consulted as work proceeds.

Definition: 
A community scholar is someone from the involved community with special expertise in one or more aspects of local culture

Key point

Think carefully about the role of the participants, and reflexively about your own role and attitudes. Some questions to consider include the following:

- How will the project affect the community?
- Are the questions being asked during fieldwork intrusive?
- Are organizers being fully realistic about what community participants can and want to do?

For example, it may not be reasonable to make plans to train community members for "new careers in the arts" when, in fact, it can be very difficult to make a living this way.

In some communities, it can be disruptive to promote the work of one member, however outstanding or excellent, because communal responsibility is often a social ideal; that is, the work itself is not about what the individual does but rather how the work contributes to the overall welfare of the community. It is very important to consider the social ramifications of the project for both the individual and the community.

Key point

Pay close attention to the varied and possibly conflicting agendas of the different individuals and groups involved in the project. The executive or board of a major cultural organization may have one agenda, its curator another, a collaborating community center another, and local ethnic leaders still others. Funders may have very different requirements and objectives. Such differing agendas can be made to work harmoniously, but only if differences are recognized and constructively negotiated. Outside experts can sometimes be called upon to provide new perspectives on concepts that are challenging, threatening, or unpopular, such as the previously mentioned concept of the community scholar.

Key point

In most community-based projects, decision making is at least partially shared. Such sharing can work surprisingly well, but it can also become contentious. On one project, a community panel was promised ultimate editorial control over the product. Then, a representative of a foundation that had decided to fund the project insisted that its participation made this arrangement null and void. The result was a project mired in resentment and endemic con- flict that dragged on for years, leaving bitterness all around.

Key point

Requesting and responding to feedback from the groups involved in or affected by a project is crucial. ***Most projects can benefit greatly from a community advisory panel with representatives from the various sectors that the project is designed to reach.*** Other community members should be consulted informally as part of the networking process. Such people need to be presented with plans and ideas early enough so that they can have time to respond before decisions are already set. Their criticisms and suggestions should inform the discussion among all those involved with the project. This form of participation takes time but is an essential part of the educational process, especially for those unfamiliar with or outside of the cultural practices of the community.

Key point

Organizing small public events that present early research results can be a useful way to communicate the project and to test community reaction. A large project that makes its only public presentations at the end of its work risks unforeseen difficulties or mistakes at the last minute (not to mention being rained out!). Even if the ultimate goal is to produce a major community event or a television program, it is wise to hold some community forums or to put a small portable photo exhibit into several local venues while the research phase is still in progress. Project personnel might consider writing an op-ed piece for the local newspaper and/or community newsletter describing the project. This approach helps to stir community interest and invite comments.

Cross Reference: See Chapter 2 in this volume regarding relationships with media

Key point

Technical assistance elements can be built into the project as essential components or products. This "gives something back" in substantial ways directly to the communities and individuals involved. The following example illustrates the reciprocal nature of technical assistance.

EXAMPLE 3.1

COLLABORATION AMONG PUBLIC RADIO, CULTURAL HERITAGE ARTS PROGRAMS, AND LOCAL ARTISTS

As part of a collaboration between Connecticut Public Radio (CPR) and the Connecticut Cultural Heritage Arts Program, five of the state's traditional music groups were professionally recorded in the radio station's studio. The recordings were incorporated into features on the musicians' ethnic communities that were produced and broadcast by CPR, and in return, the musicians received demo tapes for promotional use. Recently the studio recordings were edited into a compact disc. The Center for Traditional Music and Dance in New York City provides videotapes of their performances to guest artists in the Center's "Folk Parks" concerts. In many cases, artists have not been able to obtain these kinds of costly marketing materials, so funded projects can do a service by providing them.

CASE EXAMPLES

The three case examples that follow make use of the above principles by conducting qualitative or ethnographic fieldwork and, together with community scholars and artists, using the results to produce public programs commanding regional and statewide attention. The first case example, the "Brass Workers History Project," written by Jeremy Brecher, focuses on the conduct of an oral history project that evolved into a large multiethnic and multiyear folk festival. The second, by Ruth Glasser, describes the relationship between the ethnographer (in this case, a public historian working in the domain of ethnomusicology) and a folk festival. The third case example, by Lynne Williamson, presents an interactive exhibit and installation and fair, interwoven with related public activities highlighting the traditional art forms and contemporary circumstances of newly arrived Tibetan families in Connecticut. Each case study is followed by a checklist of considerations for using ethnography for public programming and for summarizing lessons learned.

Case Study

THE BRASS WORKERS HISTORY PROJECT[3]

Jeremy Brecher

Origins

In 1973, I finished a long book on American labor history. Even though half the period it covered was within living memory, I wrote it without talking to a single worker. I knew that there was something wrong about the process, and that there had to be a better way. If I was going to do labor history, I wanted to find or invent some way to do it that included those who had lived the experiences I was studying.

A few years later, I was invited to a party in Waterbury, Connecticut, an industrial city that was only about 30 miles from my home but that I had hardly ever visited. I had fascinating conversations with several people who had been active in the local labor movement in the 1930s. It occurred to me that perhaps Waterbury was the place to do the kind of labor history project I was trying to imagine.

Through preliminary research, I learned that the Naugatuck Valley, of which Waterbury was the principal city, had been the center of the American brass industry from the start of the 19th century through the first half of the 20th. It was still known as the Brass Valley.

I also met Jan Stackhouse and Jerry Lombardi, video documentary makers living in the Valley. Jan had been a union organizer and had coordinated the local women's center; Jerry had been active in Valley community organizations. They had made videotapes on unemployment in the Valley and on a major local brass strike, and they were interested in making a video about local labor history. Hank Murray, the education director for United Auto Workers (UAW) Region 9-A, which represented most of the unionized industrial workers in the Valley, was a friend of theirs; he suggested that we focus on a history of the brass workers in the Naugatuck Valley.

Project Goals

Through the grapevine, we learned that the National Endowment for the Humanities (NEH) was expanding its funding of labor history projects, especially those producing programs for the general public rather than just for scholars. We designed a project that we thought would appeal to them. We proposed to produce a popular book and a videotape documentary on the brass workers intended to make available to a general audience the themes developed by the "new labor history," which at that time was developing a less institutional, more cultural exploration of working-class life. We would involve workers and other community members who had lived that history, thus developing a model for workers' participation with historians and media producers in recounting their own history. Our approach grew out of our social convictions:

- We see this kind of history, not as an academic exercise, but as a social act, a way that people can communicate with each other about their experiences, needs, aspirations, and potentials.
- We believe that social movements are essential to social progress, and that those who are powerless in society need to organize and deal with their problems through collective action (Brass Workers History Project, 1982, p. 278).

In addition to the historian and two media professionals, we included a position for a community outreach person who would be responsible for taking the initiative in this area. We proposed to organize history committees in local unions, senior centers, and other organizations, and to help them preserve their own history while involving them in our project on the brass workers. Drawing on the experience of the Massachusetts History Workshop, we planned to run reunions of former brass workers. We planned to set up a Labor/Community Advisory Panel.

The Institute for Labor Education and Research in New York City, which had received previous grants from the NEH, agreed to serve as our nonprofit sponsoring organization and intermediary with the NEH. We then began a long series of revisions in response to NEH queries. During this period, we would have liked to conduct extensive discussions around the Valley to get input from worker and community groups to help shape the project. But we felt we could not justify getting people excited and involved, only to find that funding might not be forthcoming. So our initial contacts tended to be limited to higher union officials, heads of local cultural institutions, and others whose statements of support were needed for the grant application.

After many months, the NEH came through with a substantial grant. Unfortunately, it provided one less staff position than we had requested. Thus, to be able to produce the products we had promised, we had to cut out the community outreach person. The result was to introduce a continuing tension between the need both to produce high-quality products and to conduct a substantial community outreach program. The closest we came to resolving this tension was an early decision to limit our community outreach activity to that which would contribute directly to the book and documentary we had to produce, a necessary decision but one that limited the effort we could put into community activities in their own right.

Getting Started

Work on the project began in April 1980. One of our first activities was to make the rounds of local organizations that might in one way or another be affected by our activity, such as union locals and retirees chapters, senior centers, and local historical societies. These courtesy visits recognized the importance of whatever group we were approaching and allowed us to explain what we were doing before they heard about it quite possibly in distorted form from somebody else. This process laid the groundwork for future requests for help. In the case of the unions, our admission ticket was our official support from the regional office of the principal union, although we made a point of relating to locals independently where they were not on the best of terms with the regional office. Visits to historical societies and other cultural institutions allowed us both to solicit their help and to acknowledge their turf, making it clear that we were not planning to invade it. They were pleased with our plan to turn over the materials we collected to a local institution—a policy that also indicated our desire to contribute to rather than exploit the community.

Some of our best initial contacts came from going to community events sponsored by local groups. For example, at a cultural exhibit at the Lithuanian club of Waterbury, which we saw announced in the newspaper, we met many people who were to be extremely helpful over the course of the project, including a man who had been collecting old photos of the Lithuanian community for years, and who became one of our star interviewees.

On the whole, we were met with a combination of interest and reserve. We developed the philosophy that people were right to be cautious in dealing with us. After all, they had very little reason to think we were there for any reason except to rip them off, turning their lives, sufferings, and triumphs into the stuff of our own academic or media careers. We had all seen too many cases in which individuals and communities were exploited by scholars and media people, their stories taken and nothing given in return. In fact, people are often less wary of such exploitation than they should be. This attitude helped us to respond positively to people who showed signs of wariness in dealing with us, and it helped us control our own subjective anxiety in the face of lack of immediate acceptance.

I am sure that our attitudes in face-to-face situations were important to the responses we received. To the extent that we communicated interest and respect for individuals we dealt with, they, in turn, were likely to at least give us a fair hearing. To the extent that we communicated lack of respect, we turned people off. One of the clearest cases of the latter occurred when we had set up a session for a group of previously interviewed workers to be photographed. They had dressed up in their best and were looking forward to the occasion. Unfortunately, the photographer was unable to make the session and unable to call to cancel. We were told later that they had been very upset by this and had interpreted it as a sign that we did not regard them as important enough to make sure that the photographer showed up. Fortunately, this incident was unique; it would not have taken too many events of this kind to seriously undermine people's faith in our respect for them.

We learned that it took time and effort to gain people's trust. Phone calls or visits were constantly necessary to gather photos, track down interviewees, or check facts. They had the secondary benefit of telling people that we were still there, still working, and still interested in their participation, communicating our seriousness and commitment. Maintaining contact on a one-to-one basis was a time-consuming job. But over the course of 3 years, we developed a range of contacts and a depth of trust that would allow an infinitely greater degree of participation than would have been possible in the early months of the project.

The personal demands of this work were considerable. We tried to deal in a human way with the 200 or so people who became involved with the project in one manner or another. We tried not to rush when we were with people, nor to act like reporters running to file their stories, nor to schedule so many meetings and interviews that we could not be there for those with whom we talked, despite the pressure of completing the final products within tight deadlines. We had to learn to deal diplomatically with a very wide range of people and to question our own prejudices, which we were constantly discovering.

Despite several years of close contact, we were not accepted as insiders. Even those who liked and trusted us no doubt concealed some of the inside stories they might have shared with members of their own group. (The plus side of this is that we were able to relate to many different groups in the community in a way that would have been difficult for someone identified with one particular group.) The status we achieved with many people might be described as "pet outsider." As long as we did not feel a personal need for some deeper form of acceptance, this provided a very good basis for the work of the project.

We worried a lot initially about how to explain what we were doing. We knew how to describe what we wanted to do to labor historians and academically educated social activists. We had learned to present it in the unique combination of academic and populist modalities that marked the NEH of the 1970s. But neither of these presentations corresponded to either the language or the frame of reference of those with whom we would be dealing in the Valley. Indeed, they would be almost universally alien and alienating.

After many efforts to explain the project to various people, I concluded that, whatever we said, people would evaluate our behavior on the basis of their own knowledge and experience. They would decide who we were and what we were doing on the basis of that more than on the basis of what we said about ourselves.

More important, I came to the conclusion that it was all right for people to form an understanding of the project that differed from ours. Whether their idea of what we were up to coincided with our own mattered less than whether they felt they had good reasons to cooperate with us or avoid us. I believe, for example, that there were people who thought that what we were doing was silly, or that the products we talked about were mere fantasies that would never be realized, and yet they gave time and assistance to the project. In some cases, they may have done so because we were nice, idealistic young people whom they felt good about helping, in others because we listened with interest and respect to reminiscences they enjoyed sharing.

Cross Reference: See the discussion of "cover stories" for ethnographers in Book 6, Chapter 1

Over time, I came to think of introducing the project less as explaining what we were doing than as negotiating a basis for a mutually rewarding relationship. We described the project as briefly as possible, often saying little more than that we were telling the story of the brass workers and their families, that we were producing a movie and a book, and that we wanted to talk to people about their experiences. If people asked questions, we answered them frankly, but we did not go into detailed explanations unless people wanted them. This actually allowed people to focus on what about us was of interest to them, without the distraction of a long explanation, much of which they had little reason to care about. As a result, the project came to be many things to many people, something with which we learned to be comfortable.

The Valley was notoriously a place of social factionalism. Some of the past lines of cleavage we knew. The local labor movement had been the locus of severe Left/Right battles in the 1930s and 1940s, which at times had brought people who worked side by side to fisticuffs. Local politics were notorious for ethnic rivalry, and racial tensions had been high in several Valley communities. Other tensions we were unaware of and discovered only over time. For example, there was considerable rivalry among the various union locals, as well as divisions within the district between pro- and antiadministration forces. One of the locals itself was polarized into two factions, one of which had held a sit-in at the union office a few years before. All in all, we felt like we were entering a minefield.

It is easy, in a situation like this, to become socialized into and identified with one or another group. We tried to avoid this by taking the position that we were here to learn, not to take sides. We tried to be sympathetic to different positions, even to those with which we personally disagreed, on the grounds that people had reasons for their feelings and beliefs that it was our responsibility to understand, regardless of our own opinions.

Cross Reference:
See Book 6 on the ethnographer as learner

Initially, we had intended to organize reunions and group interviews. We were worried, naturally, that these might lead to sterile confrontations in which old battles would simply be relived and rehashed and that might embroil us in conflicts that would undermine our future community relations. Ultimately, we decided that we would meet with people only individually or in their own groups. (We were also careful to avoid telling people what others had been saying to us.) At the time, this seemed rather the coward's way out, but in retrospect, I think it is really a form of respect for community divisions: If people chose to be

Cross Reference:
See Book 3 for methods of conducting focused group interviews

antagonistic, it was not really appropriate for us to try to force them to change.

Of course, in a broader sense, it was part of our job to help people see their immediate experience in a larger context, and thereby to see what they had in common with people they might otherwise consider antagonists. But reconciliation could only be a result of our work, not a premise. A particularly dramatic example was the case of two men who worked closely with us who had been rank-and-file leaders on opposite sides of the Left/Right union struggle in the 1940s. After working with each of them separately for nearly 2 years, we finally decided we would risk inviting them both to a party along with several dozen other participants in the project. They initially greeted each other warily, but after the hours had passed and the liquor had flowed, we found them together in a back room, helping each other explain to a circle of younger activists seated around them why people like them had never sold out. As each of them spoke, he tapped the other on the knee and said, "As Mike will tell you" or "as Bill will tell you."

The local newspaper had a reputation for being outspokenly right wing and for attacking as radical anything it did not care for. One of the brass companies had a right-wing spokesman and a record of previous run-ins with local critics who had tried to dig up its history. Once any charges were made by this company's spokesperson, the project would be in deep trouble. We tried to avoid blatant provocations, and except for a major feature article on the project in the local paper, we kept a pretty low profile. To some extent, we were protected by the auspices under which we functioned. We were, after all, sponsored by a government agency. We also had the blessings of the UAW leadership and maintained good relations with all sections of the state labor movement.

I think what protected us the most, however, was that large numbers of people met us, talked to us, and could see with their own eyes who we were and what we were doing. That we had made the rounds of community organizations and institutions meant that we were not some mysterious invading force but people whose actions and character had been observed. I suspect that grapevine information on us was widespread, especially in labor circles, if only for its novelty value. This meant that if anybody was suspicious of us, he or she had ways to check us out other than asking the local paper to call the FBI.

Interviewing and Networking

After we had made our initial round of courtesy visits, we were somewhat awed by the problem of how to proceed with the community participation aspect of our work. We had found plenty of people who expressed some degree of interest in the project, but nobody who was ready either to start working with us on a regular basis or to organize a history committee in their own organization. We decided to push ahead with interviewing because it would allow us to get started on the products of the project; it might interest some people enough to participate further with us; and in any case, it would move us out of the office and into contact with the people with whom we were supposed to be dealing. It was a good decision, and I would advise any community history project team that feels stuck simply to go out and spend some time doing interviews.

Finding people to interview did not turn out to be a problem. We asked everyone we met to suggest people to interview, and virtually all of them came up with suggestions. We often started by interviewing our initial contact people at unions or senior centers and then asking them to arrange interviews with other members, relatives, or friends. In effect, we used the networks we had or were establishing. For most people, the fact that we came to them through a friend, relative, or acquaintance probably made a big difference in ensuring our acceptability.

Cross Reference:
See Book 2 on network sampling and in-depth sampling, and Book 4, Chapter 2, on ethnographic network research

When people said they did not know or remember enough to make it worth interviewing them, we emphasized our belief that they personally did know things that were important to us; and that even if they may not have been deeply involved with the union, we were extremely interested in what they could tell us about their work in the rolling department of the brass mill or about growing up in the North End. I would estimate that overall, more than three fourths of those we approached for interviews ultimately agreed. Those who would not talk with us no doubt had a variety of reasons for the decision. We surmise, on the basis of grapevine information, that one was suspicious that the project was more of a racket than something legitimate, and another, an oft-burned radical, preferred to keep a low profile.

We found arranging the interviews to be a tedious process. I had a personal aversion to calling strangers on the phone, which made this a high-stress activity for me. People were hard to reach on the phone. Many people would put us off and require repeated calls; perhaps this was, in part, a way of testing the seriousness of our interest. Without a reminder call the day before, few people remembered our appointments at all. And even with reminders, we had to tolerate a fair number of no-shows. Ultimately, we had to accept that we were very low on people's list of priorities. It is hard to see why we should have been otherwise.

After our first 20 or 30 interviews, we began to see the limits of our initial approach. We were very strong in those areas where we had initial contacts, such as among unionized workers and the Lithuanian community. We were also strong with people who tended to be more like ourselves: I had far more interviews with men than with women, for example.

To compensate for this, we began to put extra effort into reaching a broader cross-section of the Valley's working class. This required more work with less reward, because we lacked the pre-established networks we had in other areas. It was also more anxiety-provoking, because it meant dealing with people with whom we had less in common. But we discovered that with persistence we could find the people we needed. We defined the categories in which we were weak, and then we asked anyone we could find if they had people to suggest. A visit to the priest of the Catholic parish that served the Puerto Rican community brought us an introduction to one of the first Puerto Ricans to work in the Waterbury brass mills. A plea to a union organizer brought us to a black woman union activist whose mother had been one of the first black women to work in a company that had excluded them until World War II.

At the outset of the project, we had been offered the anthropologist's adage, "Behind every great ethnographer lies a great informant." Looking for that Great Informant was very far from my somewhat populistic notions of how to do community history, but over time, I learned that there are indeed natural historians who have an interest in and talent for the history around them, just as there are people who are good at making cars run or flowers grow. Finding them is largely a matter of chance—two of the best were uncles of people who wandered into our office in response to a newspaper article on the project. But over the course of the project, we found quite a few great informants, and they were not only exciting to talk with but gave our book and video a depth of insight that the staff could never have achieved without them.

Cross Reference:
See the discussion of key informants in Book 2, Chapters 4 and 6

All of the staff had done some interviewing before but never open-ended historical interviews with people who were not used to any public role. We had to discover the art of this kind of interviewing as we went along.[4] For me, respect is the beginning and the end of good interviewing technique. You have to regard your source as someone who is at least your equal and from whom you have a great deal to learn. If those who study working-class communities feel themselves superior to those they study, their subjects are likely to be well aware of it; reticence will be the reward for condescension or contempt.

When people agree to be interviewed, they are putting part of the meaning of their lives in your hands. They should be asked to do so only if you are willing to respect it and to guarantee that you will not degrade it, either in your personal interaction with them or in the way you use what they give you. They need to know that they will not be forced into areas they find embarrassing or uncomfortable, and that you will be sensitive enough to back away from such areas before they have to say, "I'd rather not talk about that."

We regarded the people we were interviewing as experts on the part of the world they inhabited. We were genuinely interested in what they had to tell us. This helped overcome many people's belief that, "I don't really have much that you would be interested in" or "I don't remember too much about the old days." In fact, I came to the conclusion that feelings of inadequacy were often more important in inhibiting people's participation in interviews than was anxiety about what might be revealed.

In the end, we had little difficulty getting people to talk freely. No doubt people withheld some things, and we assumed that if they did, they had good reasons for doing so. I think we were successful to the extent that we were indeed worthy of people's trust.

We did a few group discussions and interviews, and the staff learned a good deal from the back-and-forth responses. But they turned out to be rather difficult to manage; everyone wanted to talk at once and wanted others to listen to them. Even with several staff members, each trying to respond to some of the participants, the results tended to be rather unsatisfying for all. Where elderly participants were hard of hearing, the situation was aggravated. The tapes of such sessions proved extremely difficult to transcribe. Meetings with groups can still be valuable for a community history project, but we suggest that they be viewed primarily as a community activity rather than as a form of research interview.

Cross Reference: See Book 3, Chapter 2, on the conduct of focused group interviews, and for a discussion of circumstances maximizing their use

Worker/Community Participation

The worker/community participation aspect of our project was frankly experimental. We had no assurance that even a single person would be interested in working with the project in any way. Our task was difficult in itself and was almost bound to engender insecurity, tension, and self-doubt in the staff as we sat isolated in our office and tried to do something nobody really knew how to do.

One of the first things we learned was to make initial requests for participation limited. Asking someone who had never thought about it to organize a history committee in their union local was entirely inappropriate. On the other hand, asking them to be interviewed, to set up an interview with an acquaintance or family member, or to go through the box of old family photos with us was a reasonable approach that was likely to elicit a positive response.

We initially defined the project as a way that we could help people in the community tell their own history. Thus, we offered to help people do things: collect the history of their own organization, set up a history committee, or learn how to operate video equipment. We rapidly learned that most people defined participation very differently: as them helping us. I now believe that our initial approach was rather arrogant, and that theirs represented a more realistic view of the situation. Ideally, people in the community might have decided that this was their project, and we were there merely to help; but that was unlikely to occur, given the fact that the project had, in fact, been initiated by its own staff without wide community consultation. Short of that, the fact that people defined their participation as helping us allowed them rather than us to feel the pride of the giver. Perhaps that also helped make our expertise, education, and sanction from the outside society less intimidating.

We soon learned that we would not receive instant mass interest and participation in the project. For example, people were glad to let us talk briefly to their organizations' meetings, but no one offered to set up a history committee. We rapidly shifted from the idea of committees to the concept of liaison people who would connect us to various groups.

The strategy for participation that we eventually evolved was to build an informal support network around the project. We made a point of calling people we had met and asking for their opinions or help. Occasionally, we would ask someone to go on an interview with us, make a contact, or otherwise take part. Jan Stackhouse had a particular knack for this kind of relating, which proved an important asset for the project, but everyone on the staff did a large amount of such work, drawing on their individual skills and proclivities. This process was time-consuming, but its cumulative effect was substantial.

As we went along, we discovered more and more people who became interested in working with the project. A local Black poet read about us in the newspaper and walked into our office one day, eventually becoming a paid part-time staff member. A woman union activist, who initially had set up an interview for us, ended up running an old photo contest, publicizing the project up and down the Valley, and doing interviews for the project on her own. Another volunteer made excellent maps for the book that showed ethnic succession in the area.

People participated in a variety of activities, from giving an interview to organizing for the project, for many reasons. Some, particularly those who had been active in unions and ethnic organizations, felt that they had been part of something that was historically significant, something worth preserving. Others already had special interests, such as a particular neighborhood or ethnic group, and felt that they could learn more about it by working with us. A few, particularly the labor and community activists, had social messages that they felt we could help pass on to coming generations. Some were history buffs who enjoyed this kind of activity for its own sake. Some people were proud of their lives and of what they could remember, or they simply enjoyed reminiscing about old times.

Participation grew steadily with time. Over the course of several years, we met dozens of people who were interested in working with the project. At the end of 3 years, I believe we could even have succeeded with some of our more ambitious schemes, such as history committees and reunions. But there was no way we could have generated such substantial participation at the outset.

Ultimately, we had more than 200 people involved with the project in one way or another. They contributed their stories, helped line up interviews, donated photos, set up photo sessions, and helped in many other ways. As we completed rough versions of the book and documentary, dozens of people reviewed them and gave us their comments. Twenty-five people served on the project's Community/Labor Advisory Panel. This participation certainly made the results far different from what they would have been if historians and media professionals had turned out products on their own. But the forms of participation were very different from what we had initially envisioned. Instead of formal history committees in unions and community organizations or volunteers working regularly in our office, participation took the form of a myriad of fluid, informal contacts with people who helped the project in numberless specific ways.

Perhaps most important, we drew brass workers and other community members into the process of historical interpretation. In the interviews, we tried to ask people not only what happened and how they felt about it, but also why they thought those things had happened and what they thought those things meant. Our own interpretations were often corrected or deepened. For example, we initially saw our work as a labor history project; therefore, we paid inadequate attention to ethnicity. Early on in our work, an informant chided us about this, saying, "There is something you have to understand. In the old days, Waterbury was all sectioned off, and the different ethnic groups didn't mingle. If you don't pay attention to the ethnic dimension, you will never understand this community." We reluctantly accepted his point, and the integration of the ethnic dimension into our work would later be commented on as one of its greatest strengths.

Disseminating the Products

We started distributing *Brass Valley* (Brass Workers History Project, 1982), a heavily illustrated book composed primarily of oral history materials, in 1983. The book received substantial coverage in the local newspapers, and project staff gave talks about it and sold copies in local clubs and libraries. It was for sale in union halls and downtown department stores, as well as in local history museums. One young brass worker, who had written the book's preface, sold it out of his locker in the plant. In retrospect, I believe we also could have sold it in variety stores, restaurants, and other community outlets, as well as at local cultural and even sporting events, but money ran out and project staff left the area or moved on to other work before such approaches were tested. The United Auto Workers donated copies of the book to schools and libraries throughout the region. The book made enough of an impact locally that I was occasionally stopped by strangers on the street or in the library and asked about it.

So far as I can judge, reaction to the book was very positive. Many people bought it as a Christmas present, especially for older relatives and for family members who had moved away from the area. It seems to have been taken as a kind of collective family album in a community where almost everyone had a relative who worked in the brass industry. Many, many people told me that they found relatives in its pictures. One family told me that they spent Christmas together going through it. Management people who had roots in the local community liked it despite its labor orientation. We received occasional criticism for overemphasizing immigrant workers at the expense of the Yankee entrepreneurs who were "really responsible for the achievements of the brass industry"; several people quarreled with our handling of internal political conflict in the labor movement. Many readers complained that we slighted the particular department where they themselves had worked, which I took as a sign that they felt positively about the book. Other local people definitely recognized themselves in the book and were pleased to have their experiences represented.

Brass Valley,[5] a feature-length documentary video, was completed in 1984. We showed it first to a special audience of those who had been involved one way or another in the project, and then in union halls, history museums, senior organizations, and elsewhere in the Naugatuck Valley. Local reactions to the movie were strongly positive. People were very impressed that it treated their often-maligned communities with respect. Many who had worked in the factories identified strongly with the portrayal and said that we had told the truth about their experience in a way that they had never seen on television or in other media. Several people said that they had lived in the community all their lives but had never before had the pieces of its history put together for them. One elderly woman told us that her husband had worked in the brass mills all his life, but that she had never understood what he went through and the effect his work must have had on him until she saw the movie. Some people with an orientation toward the local business community regarded the movie as excessively prolabor, whereas some union officials (although none, so far as I know, in the Naugatuck Valley) regarded the movie as unsympathetic to the labor movement.

After a major press build-up, the movie was shown statewide on Labor Day evening on all of the stations of the Connecticut Public Television system. Several people told me that they heard the program being discussed at work the next morning. A few days later, on a follow-up program, "Brass Valley Counter-Point," John Driscoll, head of the

Connecticut State Labor Council AFL-CIO, and I discussed some of the issues raised by the movie, particularly its presentation of political divisions within the Naugatuck Valley unions in the 1940s (a struggle in which he was a major actor) and its general portrayal of the labor movement. The video has remained available through local organizations and is rebroadcast periodically on cable TV.

Continuing Impacts

A variety of other efforts grew out of the Brass Workers History Project. A permanent archive was established at the Mattatuck Museum in Waterbury, which has served as a resource for many subsequent activities. I prepared the text for the museum's permanent exhibit on Waterbury history, which drew heavily on materials from the Brass Workers History Project. The museum also ran a series of teacher training workshops using materials gathered by the project. Several community-based research projects have followed, such as a study of Waterbury's North End and a recently initiated oral history of the city's black community. Two other offspring, the Waterbury Ethnic Music Project and Ruth Glasser's research on Waterbury's Puerto Rican community, are described in the next section.

A couple of years after the project was completed, I wrote that the long-term impact on consciousness would be difficult to judge (Brecher, 1986, p. 276). Twelve years later, I believe that the project had a significant impact on the way people in the Valley understand its history. When we started work, the dominant explanation of why the brass industry had declined, even among brass workers, was that workers and unions had been too greedy in their demands and that as a result, the companies had left. In our products, we had provided a far more complex view, one that emphasized the process by which local brass companies had become subsidiaries of global energy corporations for whom the Valley's aging brass plants were but numbers on a balance sheet. Disinvestment in Valley factories—referred to as "milking"—was, in fact, a long-standing corporate policy that led naturally to industrial abandonment. This view has become a widespread alternative in the Naugatuck Valley, which I have heard and continue to hear repeatedly when the region's deindustrialization is discussed. It became the cornerstone of the analysis provided by a community coalition called the Naugatuck Valley Project, which brought together scores of religious, labor, and community organizations in the mid-1980s to combat plant closings.

In 1986, the workers at Seymour Manufacturing Company, one of the brass plants where we had worked most intensively, discovered that their plant was threatened with sale and/or closing. They organized to purchase and run the plant, calling their new company Seymour Specialty Wire: An Employee-Owned Company. Several of those involved in organizing the buyout had also been involved with the Brass Workers History Project. We were told by the son of a worker at the plant that, in his estimation, the appreciation for the value and significance of the plant and its heritage that developed as a result of the project had contributed to the commitment of the workers and community to saving it.

Recently, I went to a community meeting regarding the cleaning up and redevelopment of a contaminated brass mill site in Thomaston. A local resident gave an impressively detailed account of the plant and its relationship with the community over the previous century. I surmised from his talk that his family had worked there for generations. After the talk, I went up to him and asked how he came to know so much about the community's history. He told me that, indeed, he had learned much from his family and from other old-timers. But, he said, "if you really want to know about the history of this place in depth, there's a book about it you have to read. It's called *Brass Valley.*"

Of course, everything has its downside. Now, when I try to do oral history in the Valley, I always have to worry whether the accounts I get have been contaminated by the work of the Brass Workers History Project.

The following case study illustrates the ways in which reciprocal informational exchanges between community residents involved in public programming and academic historians can enrich both public programs and historical representation. The author, Ruth Glasser, is an independent historian with a special interest in ethnomusicology and the history of Puerto Ricans in Connecticut. She writes about her experience in the Waterbury Ethnic Music Festival and how that experience helped her to integrate her community organizing experience with her training and commitment to representing alternative histories to the public, especially to "publics" whose histories are not widely known, valued, or recorded. Her work also focused on the diversity within ethnic groups and an encouraging dialogue and creative exchange between ethnic groups.

Case Study

COMMUNITY AND ACADEMIC HISTORY PROJECTS: A CREATIVE INTERPLAY

Ruth Glasser

I have been a practicing public historian and cultural programmer (for want of a better term) for 11 years. My public-oriented history career started while I was in graduate school and after I had spent years participating in small (non-history-related) community organizing projects. During my time in graduate school and since, I have found that it is difficult to separate public programming from academic history, research from writing, learning from teaching. Throughout numerous projects, my community and public programming work has informed my writing and vice versa. In this section, I will talk about some valuable lessons learned from, and applicable to, the community work itself. I will also demonstrate the effects of this process of learning, discovery, and development upon my academic work, as I have gone back and forth between these different spheres of activity.

The Waterbury Ethnic Music Project

My first taste of the mutual influence of the community and the academy was in my second year of graduate school, when I joined the ranks of the Waterbury Ethnic Music Project (WEMP). Headed by Jeremy Brecher, WEMP's aim was to compile the music of the many different ethnic groups in Waterbury, a working-class town in central Connecticut. The tapes of music collected from people in their homes, social gatherings, and houses of worship were to be used for a series of programs on Connecticut Public Radio. But WEMP's effects on the larger community and even on its organizers extended far beyond that series of programs. Ultimately, the Waterbury Ethnic Music Project has led to a host of successive activities, including a series of multiethnic music festivals, ethnic curriculum packets, musicians visiting schools, and many other projects, all based on the resources of area musicians and ethnic cultural activists. What began as a seminar paper became an apprenticeship in oral and public history, leading to further community and academic work that continues to this day.

There are many reasons why the echoes of the Waterbury Ethnic Music Project have continued to reverberate throughout the region, as well as throughout my own professional life. Among the most important reasons, the project was built upon a prior effort described previously, the Brass Workers History Project. Although in 1986, I was a newcomer to the Naugatuck Valley and to WEMP, I was able to witness firsthand, and to benefit directly from, the effects of layering one project on top of another. ***As one who has since had both short- and long-term fieldwork experiences, I cannot overemphasize the value of being in an area for the long haul.*** Entering and leaving a community quickly to complete fieldwork, finish one's project, and then go on to something else somewhere else is certainly possible and often seems inevitable in these days of limited time and grant money. But to me, it feels like the moral and emotional equivalent of strip-mining. It is not nearly as rewarding either personally or to the fieldwork community as

Key point

staying in the area and doing a series of projects in the same place. Many of the contacts needed for the Music Project, for example, were derived from the Brass Workers Project, and the networks broadened and deepened over time. When WEMP project staff decided to establish the Waterbury Traditional Music Festival (later the Brass Valley Ethnic Music Festival), we, as researchers and programmers, as well as the concept of what we were doing, were at least somewhat familiar to many community members.

Key point *Patience was critical in our work.* It is only in retrospect, however, that I think WEMP researchers and programmers realized the enormous amount of patience and time that we needed to accomplish our most important goals. The patience, time, and goals I speak of are not the short-term variety—of 90-hour work weeks, for example, invested over a series of weeks or months to win an organizing campaign. They are of more modest, undramatic, long-term and abstract varieties. Some of the means to reach these goals evolved slowly or are still developing.

Building Multiethnic Dialogue and Affirming Local Cultural Resources: A Project Goal

From the beginning, it was important to us that our projects foster a creative dialogue among groups of people at best isolated from one another, and at worst hostile to each other, within this small city. The radio shows and the festivals were unabashedly multicultural, long before "multicultural" was a ubiquitous buzzword. They compared and mixed the music of the city's many ethnic and racial groups.

The programs, festivals, and ensuing activities were also meant to be strong affirmations of the value of the cultural resources of the local community. Waterbury was a swiftly deindustrializing town whose local resource had been the brass industry. It had no major university or white-collar sector. The working class and elites alike tended to characterize the city as having "no culture." Rather than going along with would-be Waterbury revitalizers' notions that the city needed to import culture—more opera, theater, big rock stars, and so on—our projects aimed to show that Waterbury already had culture. Listeners to the radio programs, for example, might learn for the first time that their city had French or Cape Verdean clubs with their own events, that the Puerto Rican community had its own dedicated cultural activists, or that Albanian and African American musicians from Waterbury all struggled to make a living at their art. Our festivals featured local acts only, chosen with the help of a multiethnic steering committee of local people. There were no big names brought in from out of town, in stark contrast to all of the other festivals we had heard of at the time.

But the multiethnic theme actually took years to catch on with Waterbury audiences, and that is where time, patience, and slow development of goal-reaching processes come in. During the first festival, for example, members of different groups came largely to hear members of their own ethnic group sing or play. Only by virtue of scheduling glitches (e.g., no time between acts to rearrange the stage) did people inadvertently find themselves listening to groups different from themselves. Over the years, however, while we both improved our logistical organizing and learned to appeal to audiences of different ages and tastes, our audiences and musicians began to look forward to listening to and jamming with each other. These lessons could be learned only over time and with repeated festivals.

The Importance of Sympathetic Funders

One of the reasons that ongoing spinoffs and outgrowths from both the Brass Workers Project and the Music Project have been possible is because of sympathetic local funding sources, particularly the Connecticut Humanities Council and the Connecticut Council on the Arts. All too often, it is unfashionable in grant circles to continue to focus on an area that has been "done" already. ***Having local funders who regard ongoing research and public programming in the same geographic areas as a good investment gives public***

Key point

programmers the time they need to see the long-term and profound effects of their work on local communities and community building.

All of this is not to suggest a permanent condition of financial success and programmatic satisfaction. For example, over time, it became impossible to sustain the festival at the same level, precisely because of the amounts of time and money required to organize it. Neither programmers/ scholars nor museum personnel could continue donating their own time and resources at the same level, and it was difficult to pass it on as a project to already overburdened cultural activists. Local grant agencies could not provide the level of funding needed to maintain the festival. Over time, national sources considered the festival as having been "done." ***The development of working partnerships is another critical component of public programming.*** In this instance, it helped to stabilize some key features of the festival, even without large amounts of public and private funding.

Cross Reference with Key point: See Book 6, see chapter on building research partnerships

The Importance of Partnerships for Project Growth and Continuity

Key point

Collaboration between researchers, programmers, and sympathetic local institutions is indispensable in both initiating and stabilizing public programs such as folk festivals. The Mattatuck Museum, Waterbury's local art and history museum, increasingly viewed itself as having obligations to a diverse economic and ethnic community. It sponsored and continues to sponsor many of the projects mentioned previously, contributing hundreds of hours of staff time to our projects and generating its own often-related efforts.

With partnership and years of experience, a dynamic was set in motion that has continued to produce results on a somewhat smaller but persistent scale. We and the museum continued to work together to produce a series of smaller products and events: a set of fifth-grade curriculum packets based on the lives and heritages of Waterbury musicians, and a series of nights sponsoring multiethnic musical performances. When the museum organized an exhibit and series of programs revolving around multiethnic wedding traditions, a local department store willingly gave space, and local people came forth with their wedding outfits, photos, and stories. Although the museum could not completely shed its long-standing image as the bastion of the local white elite, Latino and African American cultural organizers now came through its doors. Latino cultural groups now use the museum as a base for their own performances, events, and classes. African American community leaders are collaborating with museum programming staff, with ourselves as advisors, to produce the Waterbury African American Oral History Project.

Scholarly Work Informs Public Programming

From the moment I entered the Waterbury Ethnic Music Project, my professional and scholarly fate was tied to the developments already described. In addition to learning the ins and outs of oral history and writing a seminar paper, for example, I found myself designing a radio show and directing the first Waterbury Ethnic Music Festival. The insights gained from these public activities in turn powered my more academic work. Quite simply, I owe many of the themes and methods of my academic career to the people of Waterbury—their thoughts, differences of opinion, questions, inspirations, and ideas for how to conduct fieldwork.

As a field-worker trained in historical methodology, I did not come to the project with a hypothesis I wished to test. Part of being an oral/public historian, as I quickly learned, meant maintaining an open mind, constantly examining my own prejudices, and listening deeply to interviewees in order to assimilate new ideas. If I had come to the field with a fixed idea of what ethnic music meant, for example, the first event I attended in Waterbury would have been a complete loss. Entering the social hall of Waterbury's Lithuanian section to attend a dance, I did not hear anything remotely resembling what I imagined to be local traditional Lithuanian music. What I heard, instead, was an imported orchestra playing Glenn Miller and other favorites of the Big Band era. Close questioning of audience members, however, indicated why this was the music closest to their hearts. As second-generation Americans, they grew up as American teenagers in an era where social pressures to Americanize were extremely strong. The music they had danced and romanced to as adolescents and young adults—music popular among youth across the country—was exactly that music played at the Lithuanian club dance. Interspersed with this music, however, were some polkas and *obereks*—the dance music of their parents' generation, the music that they had listened to since childhood at family events, weddings, and church celebrations. Such experiences demonstrate that people juxtapose or integrate rather than choose between ethnic traditions, holding onto their ethnic heritage while blending into a larger national culture.

Our musical informants and the members of the multiethnic festival advisory committee also argued over what, to them, was authentic music, and what best represented their ethnic communities. Each festival became a delicate balancing act both among the musical traditions of many different ethnic groups and across the different genres represented within each ethnic group. When African American community members, for example, criticized one festival's focus on gospel music, claiming that spirituals were more authentic black music, the committee was attentive, and the next festival included spirituals on the roster.

Experiences in Public Programming Can Influence Scholarly Research

If public programming can benefit from scholarly field research conducted in a collaborative manner in local settings, then scholarly field research can also benefit from and become enriched by the experiences of public programming. One important area of interactive learning stemmed from recognizing the importance of intraethnic differences in music and cultural interpretation. For the festivals, for example, we drew a wide circle around community factions and differences of opinion, learning what they were and accommodating as many as possible. Likewise, it was possible to use these apparent contradictions to drive scholarly research, rather than attempting to ignore or eliminate them because they did not fit into a preconceived research model. *My Music Is My Flag,* a social history of Puerto Rican musicians in New York City in the 1920s and 1930s (Glasser, 1995), drew upon many of the lessons we had learned about the complexity of ethnicity and the lives of musicians while working on the Waterbury festivals and other WEMP outgrowths.

Fieldwork can be considered as much more than doing the work necessary to complete a piece of writing; and learning from informants or community experts can and should go beyond their responses to the researcher's questions or the researcher's observations about them. For me, a new phase of intellectual exchange with the local community began out of a practical need. Working within WEMP and then on the music festivals showed me how to involve people in the planning and execution of public programming and how to apply those skills to my own research. When I began the work intended to lead to a public-oriented book on Puerto Ricans in Connecticut, I not only had research skills in hand but also knew how to build on prior contacts to engage in networking to locate oral history respondents. Through the Waterbury work, I had developed a philosophy that enabled me to avoid treating the "Puerto Rican community" as a monolith and compelled me to look for life experiences from many different class, race, political, religious, cultural, and geographic perspectives.

Cross Reference: See Book 6 on how to be an ethnographic learner

Nevertheless, in my research and writing, I felt the burden of loneliness. I began to ask community residents for fieldwork advice because I did not feel that my own thinking was sufficiently broad. I was rewarded magnificently. For example, I worried about how to deal with confidentiality and bringing up sensitive issues in my book, such as intimate family matters that illustrated a point, or descriptions of people engaged in the underground economy that was part of the historical picture I wished to portray in the book. I brought this up with friends in a small town in Puerto Rico. They pondered the problem, agreed that it was important to include the information, and suggested ways in which the ideas could be presented using culturally appropriate generalities rather than names. I saw that by consulting with the people I was interviewing, I could accomplish several things at once. First, it was clear that I was secure enough in my role as scholar/researcher that I could admit that I did not have all the answers. This made people feel more comfortable with me. Asking their advice became both useful to me and a meaningful way to involve and invest community residents in the projects I had undertaken to do.

At times, informants have caught me by surprise. For example, one couple called me on the carpet and asked why my work included their working-class struggles but not their children's middle-class successes. Another day, as I was getting nowhere interviewing an elderly woman, her son, who was watching, told me that I should be asking her about her efforts to raise her children as a single mother, rather than about her community and church activities. I have also asked informants to critique my manuscripts and suggest new directions and interviewees. One young Waterbury Puerto Rican informant traded his desire to learn about oral history and program planning for entry to his sector of the community. Together, we would discuss the project—whom to interview and why. He introduced me to the adults he had known all his life, and together, we interviewed them.

The next case study illustrates important challenges and dilemmas likely to confront public historians, folklorists, and social scientists, especially those working from an independent or consultant base. Dr. Glasser reminds us that graduate students can play critical roles in community-based public programming. Public programs are generally underfunded, so graduate students involved in service learning programs and internships can contribute significantly to the success of a program—learning while they gain experience as researchers and organizers.

Public programming requires careful attention to scheduling and organizing because all of the components of an event must be prepared in a timely fashion in advance in order to make it possible for the event to be "assembled" at the scheduled time. The support of community collaborators in such an event makes it possible for the ethnographer as cultural historian to partner in the production of written materials and the coordination of exhibits, performances, and other materials central to the activity.

Public projects and the programs they support are usually funded by grants. It is very important to be clear initially that funding may not be available to continue projects in the future, and that community support will be required to advocate for funding continuity, new sources of funding, or program continuity through the support of other agencies or community partnerships.

Finally, Dr. Glasser's experience illustrates the continuities and discrepancies between the worlds of academic scholarship and public programming and advocacy. Participatory scholarship represents one way of resolving the contradiction; integrating scholarship into public programming is another. Balancing both is important. To do so requires continuous presence in the community and maintenance of close personal relationships and dialogue with a broad spectrum of community scholars and residents. These are the most important elements contributing to the public programmer's ability to facilitate accurate representation of a community's perspectives.

Both of these case studies discuss the uses of ethnography in association with the public portrayal of industrial history and the creation of multiethnic music and other forms of cultural programming. In both of these instances, the authors are independent public historians who have created community partnerships and have found funding sources that have enabled them to contribute their skills as ethnographers and historians to community education efforts. The field of public folk arts and folklore is still relatively new, and some of the most creative cultural workers make their skills available as independent consultants. As independent consultants, they can define the direction of their work, choose their partners, and work toward public representation of their work without having to address the constraints that could be presented by their institutional "homes" or bases. Their primary constraints have to do with accessing resources—in particular, funding and time—and making sure that the public programming that stems from their work is supported by local presenting venues.

Other ethnographers doing similar work are based in museums, state agencies, and independent nonprofit organizations, each of which is a different kind of environment with somewhat different advantages and constraints. In the following case example, Lynne Williamson writes from her base as director of the Connecticut Cultural Heritage Arts Program of the Institute for Community Research. The Institute for Community Research is an independent, nonprofit, community-based research organization with a commitment to building research partnerships with communities and other nonprofit organizations in order to conduct better research, and making sure the results are used. The Cultural Heritage Arts Program at the Institute serves the cultural communities of the state and region in three main ways: by identifying and supporting heritage artists, by building a public archive of their work through conducting fieldwork in their communities, and working together with community scholars and artists to present their work in culturally appropriate ways.

In this case study, ethnography is used to frame a project that illustrates the material and spiritual culture of a single ethnic group in Connecticut. Following is a description of the formation, funding, and programming of the 1996 exhibition project, "Auspicious Signs: Tibetan Arts in New England," a project conducted in partnership with the local Tibetan refugee community.

AUSPICIOUS SIGNS: TIBETAN ARTS IN NEW ENGLAND

Lynne Williamson

Case Study

The work of the Institute for Community Research in Hartford, Connecticut, emphasizes the use of original research to strengthen community-based resources and affect policy and social change. As director of ICR's Connecticut Cultural Heritage Arts Program (CHAP), I developed the exhibition project, "Auspicious Signs: Tibetan Arts in New England," along with members of the local Tibetan refugee community who had expressed interest in presenting their cultural traditions in a public setting. The exhibit opening and a day-long festival served as the major public events resulting from an 18-month research and planning period. Although the exhibit closed in November 1996, our relationship with the community and individual artists continues through offering technical assistance, exhibition and performance opportunities, and social support, especially because many Tibetans are now eligible to seek citizenship after 5 years of U.S. residency.

The project was funded by grants from the Lila Wallace Readers Digest Community Folklife Program, the National Endowment for the Arts Folk and Traditional Arts Program, the Connecticut Commission on the Arts, and the Connecticut Humanities Council. Securing these varied resources was important to the construction of the project because each funder underwrote different components. These components—fieldwork and documentation, public presentation, technical assistance to artists, and publication of research—reflect the cornerstone activities of CHAP, which serves as the statewide folklife program, with a commitment to supporting the work of traditional artists and to disseminating information about this work. Also, the project's various components reflected multifaceted aspects of the Tibetan community, giving a full picture of its interests, activities, and complexities and enhancing its potential for reaching different audiences—an often-expressed goal of many Tibetans in Connecticut.

Project Goals

Project goals centered around fieldwork, communicating the results of this research to public audiences, introducing economic opportunities to Tibetans, and presenting Tibetan artists in public events so that Connecticut residents could meet members of this rapidly growing local immigrant group. A key goal of the project was to involve Tibetans in all stages of the process, especially the planning. This was geared to ensuring that the presentation honored their cultural character and communicated this clearly and accurately to the public, and that their stated interests could be achieved. Specifically, the project developed the following objectives:

- Involve members of New England Tibetan communities, especially those in Connecticut, in project planning and implementation so that they could learn how to organize and present public programs in the United States. The aim was to encourage, support, and guide community members so that the knowledge of presentation skills became theirs. For this group, in the United States only since 1992, language and American social economic systems initially presented numerous hurdles as they sought to establish employment, education, and cultural opportunities for themselves.

- Increase understanding about Tibetan culture for public audiences generally unfamiliar with this group recently settled in Connecticut, and so often appearing in current media headlines.
- Showcase the work of traditional Tibetan artists who make everyday or more utilitarian arts, as well as the better-known religious art forms.
- Support preservation of the skills and knowledge of traditional artists by providing various forms of technical assistance so that they could continue to produce their work.
- Cultivate new networks of presenting organizations and individuals interested in Tibetan culture in order to increase opportunities for Tibetan artists to participate in other regional projects and performances.

The collaborative project team consisted of three Tibetan assistants; exhibit designer Sarah Buie; the Tibetan Association of Connecticut; artist Sonam Lama, who was, at the time, vice president of the Massachusetts Tibetan Association; and myself as curator/folklorist. The interdisciplinary nature of the team served to broaden the project's outreach to regional Tibetan communities as well as incorporate a rich variety of expertise and perspectives.

The Tibetans on the team were instrumental in ensuring the authentic and appropriate character of all aspects of the project, and they provided invaluable links and contacts with Tibetan communities throughout the region. All were paid consultant fees. Artist Jampa Tsondue, president of the Connecticut Tibetan Association at the time, assisted with the exhibit and catalogue by locating photographs, offering detailed information about art techniques and the religious significance of Buddhist symbols, and collaborating on writing label texts. Musician Lakedhen Shingsur helped to organize the performances, and he expanded his role by networking extensively with Tibetans regionally, especially in New York, arranging for their Tibetan dance group to perform. Businessman Bhumba coordinated the Festival bazaar and negotiated with Tibetan stores in New York City to purchase materials such as prayer flags and butter lamps that were used in the exhibit design. In return, by working closely with project organizers, the Tibetans learned some of the steps needed to make a complex project like this happen in the United States. Especially new to them were the areas of publicity and promotion, as well as outreach to audiences beyond a single ethnic group or geographic area.

Project Fieldwork

I began compiling names of possible artists in the Tibetan community in early 1995 after meeting *thangka* painter Kalsang Jorden in New Haven in 1994. With his help, and with assistance from David Brown of the Tibetan Cultural Center of Connecticut (a group instrumental in the 1992 resettlement of Tibetans in this state), we located and interviewed seven artists, traveling to their homes in Connecticut and Massachusetts. I also attended a number of rehearsals of the local dance group and a community celebration in Old Saybrook, where most Tibetans had settled. At this last event, I met the singer DaDon, recently arrived from Tibet, and included her in the interview process. These interviews were recorded on cassette tape and, along with documentary photographs, are housed in CHAP's archive. The artists provided valuable information on their backgrounds and families, how they learned their art forms, details of techniques and methods they used, how the art expressed and was influenced by other cultural practices, and how they viewed themselves as both individual artists and community tradition bearers. CHAP's involvement in the fieldwork phase aimed to dig deep to understand the history, contexts, and contemporary realities of Connecticut Tibetans. ***This example illustrates ways in which ethnographic data are collected, as well as how the data serve to record the history and experience of a group for the group itself, for representation purposes, and for the historical record.***

Key point

Even in a community as small, geographically concentrated, and politically cohesive as the newly arrived Tibetans in Connecticut (most initially lived in or near Old Saybrook, and all deeply revere the Dalai Lama and support political and cultural independence for Tibet), internal social divisions exist. The 1,000 Tibetans who emigrated to the United States from India and Nepal in 1992 were chosen by lottery; they were not related to, nor did they necessarily know, each other. They had to negotiate social relations within their own cultural group as well as with Americans and other ethnic and national communities in the United States. Internal community differences affected the project on occasion. For example, a master carpet weaver living in Old Saybrook related that she was discouraged from contacting CHAP by others in the community. I did not manage to learn about this weaver's skills in the course of fieldwork research. Only after the exhibit ended did this weaver contact CHAP, and since then she has been included in recent programs and technical assistance initiatives. Another reason for her reticence may have stemmed from an uncertain immigration status. The situation underscores the reality that ***no matter how interested in or closely involved with a group he or she is, a researcher will not always understand or be aware of the group's internal dynamics, especially problematic tensions.*** Also, as in this case, the community may find it intrusive and embarrassing if the researcher investigates the reasons for these tensions, even when the intention is to gain greater understanding of community dynamics. ***In such instances, a long-term, trusting relationship with the community in question is the best way to come to understand and appreciate internal differences in perspective.***

Key point

Key point

Project Exhibit

Drawing upon previous successful collaborations, CHAP included a designer as a key member of the project team. Sarah Buie is head of the Graphic Design section of the Fine Arts Department at Clark University in Worcester, Massachusetts. She is an experienced exhibition designer with a long-standing interest in the cultures of India, Nepal, and Tibet, and she has traveled extensively in these countries. She worked with the Tibetan Resettlement Project in Connecticut as the Tibetans began to arrive in 1992, becoming acquainted with several of the new community's artists. Her concept for the exhibit design developed from her understanding of Tibetan Buddhist aesthetics as well as familiarity with the artists and the works they wished to exhibit. As a centerpiece in the 800-square-foot gallery, placed beneath the room's domed ceiling (painted a deep blue reminiscent of the Himalayan sky), stonemason Sonam Lama built a 900-lb. *chorten* (stupa) dedicated to the deity Namgyal. After the exhibit ended, he planned to take it back to his home community of Greenfield, Massachusetts, to install it in the new Buddhist center there.

In various ways, the three assistants helped locate materials, select and transport artworks, and install the show. They also provided information and reviewed drafts for all label texts. Sonam Lama borrowed a carpet that was made by a Tibetan weaver from New Hampshire, who was then invited to join the project. The day before the opening, one of the artists previewing the exhibit expressed unease with a painting that depicted a mythical beast. He felt it suggested a dragon—the symbol of China, Tibet's occupier. Although Kalsang Jorden, the painter, never intended any reference to China, the fact that a member of the community was genuinely troubled by the piece required us to remove it. Another painting by Kalsang was found to take its place, luckily fitting into the frame custom made for the first one.

The Festival

To mark the exhibit opening, a festival organized by CHAP and the Tibetans was held at the Institute for Community Research; it was attended by more than 300 people, including Tibetans from all over the region. Four Tibetan music and dance groups performed outside, while in the ICR gallery space, three of the exhibited artists demonstrated weaving, woodcarving, and *thangka* painting. A number of Tibetan vendors set up tables with a great variety of Tibetan books and crafts. Lakedhen and five other community members had risen at dawn to prepare Tibetan food, which they sold during the day. Several speakers introduced the background of the project, the story of the Connecticut community, the current political situation in Tibet, and the history and character of Tibetan culture. The event was free.

Key point

The interaction between community participants and the audience during a public programming event is very important because it is through interaction that groups and individuals come to learn from one another. In this instance, audience and participant interactions at the festival were constant and meaningful. Members of the public were able to meet Tibetans as people and talk to them—language difficulties did not seem to hinder communication or enjoyment. Bhumba checked with the bazaar vendors throughout the day to be sure they were successful in making sales. There was a lot of activity around the many tables, which, because of ICR's limited space, were placed close together. This was good for business because audience members *had* to pass by the vendors. Traders were pleased with their sales, which was gratifying because many had traveled to Hartford from quite a distance.

The Catalogue

The project team also produced a 28-page catalogue because the beauty of the art and the richness of traditions underpinning it warranted full presentation (Williamson, 1996). Fieldwork done with the community served as the basis for the photographs, text, and quotes, which, like the exhibit labels, were discussed in detail and reviewed by the artists (see Serrell, 1996, for more information on exhibit labels). In addition to profiles of six Tibetan artists, exhibit designer Sarah Buie contributed an essay on Tibetan aesthetics and material culture, and Peter Harle, a young folklore scholar from Indiana University, described his research on food traditions in the large Bloomington Tibetan community. ***A catalogue can help a project live on, and it also serves a valuable function because artists can use it in promoting their work.***

Key point

The Videos

During the festival, videographer and folklorist Winifred Lambrecht recorded footage of the performances and artist demonstrations. This unedited footage is housed in ICR's traditional arts archive, available to scholars and the public at any time for viewing and study. Support from the National Endowment for the Arts enabled additional videotaping at the homes of weaver Tsering Yangzon, woodcarver Ngawang Choedar, and *thangka* painter Jampa Tsondue as they worked on their art. Dr. Lambrecht edited this material into "demo" videos for the artists to use as they wished for educational or promotional purposes. The extensive raw footage of the artists at work is also available in the archive.

Technical Assistance

The project was designed to offer technical assistance to artists and the community in a variety of ways. Project assistant and flute player Lakedhen Shingsur recorded several songs in the Connecticut Public Radio Studio as part of a broadcast series on Connecticut traditional musicians. From these recordings, a demonstration tape was produced for him, and the recorded music was featured in the videos mentioned previously. Professional photos of the artists and their work that were taken for portrayal in the catalogue are also used by the artists as publicity materials.

Because Tsering Yangzom was able to bring from Nepal only a backstrap loom for belts, the project purchased a loom from Nepal for her to use in making blankets and aprons. This proved rather difficult to arrange, because the loom had to be bought and then shipped to us in Connecticut, but Dzi Tibet Collection, an import company in Washington, DC specializing in Tibetan crafts, offered assistance, and the loom arrived in time. The project also covered the cost of a second loom, a smaller model of a carpet loom, which was built in Connecticut by Kebabian's Carpet House in New Haven. Master carpet weaver Tsultim Lama, now living in Connecticut, joined exhibit artists Phurbu Kyipa from New Hampshire and Tsering Yangzom to demonstrate Tibetan weaving at the International Festival of Arts in New Haven in June 1997.

The technical assistance aspect of the project continues through two additional CHAP initiatives. A 1997 NEA-funded workshop led by economic development specialists focused on self-presentation and small business incubation for traditional artists, followed by small regrants to selected artists including Jampa Tsondue, for creating promotional brochures. The feasibility of developing products with Connecticut-based traditional artists is now being explored in a collaboration with Aid to Artisans, a Connecticut-based nonprofit dedicated to creating economic opportunities for crafts-people around the world.

Evaluation

Members of the project team found this project to be unusually successful in outcome and enjoyable to produce. This is due in large part to the extensive participation of our Tibetan colleagues, who believed they had a stake in the project and helped accordingly to make it happen. Their knowledge and dedicated assistance, as well as the experience of other project consultants, ensured the quality of our productions. The project illustrated the strengths derived from involving members of communities deeply in projects to achieve the most authentic and meaningful results, both

Key point

for participants and for the public. ***Locating and encouraging those community members who have a drive to educate or communicate about their group is crucial,*** because they will have the commitment to follow through. Their networking skills within their own community are invaluable and cannot be duplicated by outsiders, no matter how well intentioned. There is little long-term benefit in overorganizing or doing things "for" a group, because it prevents them from gaining knowledge for themselves.

Participating Tibetans most often mentioned increasing the public's understanding of their own culture and concerns as the greatest benefit of the project. They created a sense of excitement and value around the project, and this became the most effective way to network, communicate goals, and build audiences. An additional event, organized during the course of the project, was developed by members of the Tibetan community themselves. Project assistant Lakedhen Shingsur, who is deeply committed to increasing public awareness of Tibet's current political situation, urged CHAP to provide a forum for an important speaker on human rights issues. Palden Gyatso, an elderly Buddhist monk who had been imprisoned in Tibet by the Chinese for 30 years, spoke at a June 1996 public event held in ICR's gallery, surrounded by Tibetan weavings, woodcarvings, prayer flags, and *thangka* paintings. He gave a moving account of isolation and torture during his years in prison, but the most lasting impression for the large audience was of this man's compassion in the face of inhuman treatment. No exhibit label could express a central Buddhist philosophy so powerfully.

Key point

Networking is critical to successful brokering of community interests with the wider public. Networking was the heart and soul of this project, proceeding along two routes: an informal and independent one already existing among area Tibetans, and a growing network of organizations and individuals interested in Tibetan issues. One contribution of the project was to link these two networks, which resulted in wide dissemination of information about the project and the community, cultivated a very diverse audience, and increased opportunities for the Tibetans to participate in other initiatives. Other agencies that learned about the artists through the project and involved them later on include the following:

- The Asian-American Center and the Jorgensen Theater at the University of Connecticut
- The University of Massachusetts Department of Asian Music and Dance
- The New England Folklife Center in Lowell, Massachusetts
- The Peabody Museum of Natural History at Yale
- Trinity College in Hartford
- Quinipiac College in Hamden, Connecticut
- The International Festival of Arts and Ideas in New Haven
- Several Connecticut schools

In addition, Tibetan artists have been involved in a number of smaller events and presentations around New England.

A central project goal was to show Tibetan artists that their work is valued here in the United States, and that they can continue to practice their traditional arts even while making their new lives in this society. The intense pressure Tibetans feel to make money to bring their families over from India and Nepal cannot be overemphasized; many hold several jobs. They valued the project because it (rightly) paid them for their time and hard work. ***An important consideration, often ignored or forgotten, is the need to pay artists and community members for their performances or time spent working on a project.*** As a result of the project, the artists have gained more confidence in asking for reasonable honoraria. Tibetans in the region have been able to expand their opportunities to perform, exhibit, or sell their work more widely.

Key point

Because the project was spread over 2 years, it taught us an important lesson—that ***one's work with the community develops, grows, changes, and benefits from long-term commitment.*** Even though it officially ended in late 1997, the project continues through CHAP's participation in the lives

Key point

of many of those involved. Many of the Tibetans become eligible in 1998 to apply for citizenship, so the Cultural Heritage Arts Program will assist with related paperwork and requirements as well as with the bureaucratic intricacies of bringing family members to the United States. Maintaining a personal connection and relationship with people beyond the requirements of a project shows a warm and human enjoyment and concern and also helps to build trust.

A number of artists seeking residency permits as "artists of exceptional merit" have asked for support letters to be written to immigration authorities. In Connecticut, there have been marriages, artists moving into the state, many families coming over from India, some social problems solved, and many personal triumphs such as buying a house. These events mark the everyday process of their lives that it is an honor to share. Our long-term work with Tibetans makes us a better advocate for them. We definitely intend to continue our social and artistic contacts with this growing community, having learned that building trust is important overall as the first and ongoing task, whereas patience (with persistence) over the long haul is often the best way to support the preservation of traditional arts and culture for those recently arrived and living in a new and often uncomfortable environment.

CONCLUSIONS

Ethnographers have always been involved in public programming because of their affiliation with museums and their interest in the production of films and videos representing the communities and constituencies with whom they conduct their research. The nature of public programming and the growth of the field have paralleled changes in the way scholars and the public view ethnography. Ethnographers no longer can assume the right to portray communities from the researcher's point of view. Many ethnographers and historians have addressed new ways of working with communities to portray multiple voices and perspectives, sometimes leaving the readers to come to their own conclusions or, as in the case of the Brass Work- ers History Project, constructing a dialogue which included alternative perspectives based on broader analytical frames of reference from both inside and outside the group.

Public programming is assertive in its use of ethnographic research methods to portray the complexity of a culture or community to a broad public in ways that are actively supported and promoted by members of that community. Public programming extends the obligation of the ethnographer to ensure the most complete and authentic representation of one or more communities. Public programs present material, art forms, and other cultural representations through popular publications and catalogues, exhibitions, ethnic folk festivals and fairs, lectures and talks by university and community scholars and cultural experts, performances, and oral tradition. Radio, television, gallery events, festivals, and other public settings are the venues through which public programming takes place.

The teams that are responsible for public programs must be accomplished in a variety of different domains: ethnographic research; the ability to build relationships with partner communities; the identification of and negotiation for the opportunity to display, exhibit, or promote appropriate cultural forms to the public; the ability to negotiate proper venues for performance or exhibit; the capacity to write accompanying documentation for the public; and the ability to market, promote, or otherwise organize the advertisement of events to the public. All of these skills are necessary to mount a good public program. Usually, they require a team, because most individuals cannot do all of these things equally well.

When mounting public programs, the following are important considerations to keep in mind:

Things to Consider When Mounting Public Programs

- Enter an unfamiliar community through personal contacts.
- Commit to longer- rather than shorter-term residence in an area so that projects and networks can build on each other.
- Make sure that the overall goals and products expected from your project are clear and transparent, and communicate them in multiple ways.
- Whenever possible, build the project together with people in the community from the beginning; if this is not possible, make sure to build in the time and flexibility to share ownership with community partners after the fact.
- Use oral histories and other interviews as a means of extending your network of contacts while letting people know that their views are of critical importance to the project.
- Make sure that your project represents the diversity of interests and groups in the community.
- Find the people in the community to be represented who can be partners in the project. Make sure that these partners have a strong commitment to communicate with and educate others, thus maximizing the public aspects of the program for their own community.
- Make sure that your project is ethnically and culturally inclusive and sensitive to the diversity within an ethnic community.
- Retain awareness of the multiple goals and objectives of the various parties to your project.
- Respond to the needs of the community if people ask for technical assistance in an area where you can help.
- Respect the views and inputs of everyone in the community, and try to make everyone feel included.
- Remain respectful of intracommunity differences or actions. Stay on good terms with all sides, and avoid involvements in disputes. Doing otherwise might make things worse.
- Maintain realistic expectations of community volunteers. Discover what they can give. Do not assume it.

- Pay community scholars and experts for their contribution; partnership includes revenue and cost-sharing.
- Present cultural expressions the way the group "lives" them, even if this seems not to fit preconceived notions of traditionality or authenticity.
- Share results of the research with formal and informal groups within the community as the project proceeds. Do not wait till the end.
- Make sure that the public programming products—written, audiovisual, or otherwise—have been reviewed by community audiences prior to release.
- Try to make the public products available to the widest possible public using a variety of different venues and channels.
- If using the data collection process for a public program for scholarly work as well, make sure your partners are aware of this dual objective and are willing to support it.
- Build one project on the base of another, expanding on existing contacts and positive experiences.
- Recognize that the tensions between the participatory nature of public programming and the independent nature of traditional scholarly work are not easily resolved, and that resolution requires finding ways of including the public in the development of scholarly publications and documentaries as, for example, thinkers and planners, reviewers, and writers of source materials.
- Spend time with people.
- Make sure that public programming appeals to all of the senses, including intuition, by offering an array of experiences that encompasses sound, smell, taste, emotion, physical sensation, and cognitive excitement.

The strength of ethnographically informed public programming is that it is rooted in culture. This central frame of reference has two critical components: first, the culture of individual social/ethnic and national groups, which can and should be represented so that they can be appreciated both by their members and by others who learn about them; and second, the relationship **among** cultural and national groups that are also, and equally, a part of our national heritage (Williamson, 1994; 1995). We might go so far as to say that one of the primary purposes of ethnographically informed public programming is to promote dialogue both within and among cultural groups, and that an important way of doing so is by the public sharing of cultural heritage. Authentic public sharing requires a level playing field on which each ethnic or cultural group is confident about its ability to portray or represent itself appropriately (Schensul, 1990). It may take time and support for some groups to reach that point. For this reason, we recommend that public programmers take into consideration the readiness of any group to represent itself beyond the boundaries of its own reference group and provide, as a priority, the support that each group needs to hold its own in public discussions about culture, race, ethnicity, and representation (Williamson & Glasser, 1997).

We conclude with the belief that one of the best ways to come to understand another culture is to experience it through all the senses. An important role for public programming is to represent through re-creation critical elements of the culture in question so that those who attend public events can experience the culture directly. This means offering exposure to food, music, movement such as dance or games, and, most importantly, dialogue with members of the cultural group. The opportunities to encounter the unfamiliar in a safe space; ask questions; share ideas and experiences; taste, smell, and touch through performance, discussion, exhibition, and installation—these are the unique and most important dimensions of ethnographically informed public programming.

NOTES

1. The Institute for Community Research (ICR) is an independent, nonprofit, applied research center that integrates ethnography with training, public and heritage arts programming and a community arts gallery, public

discussions, dialogues, and conferences for the dissemination of research results.

2. In 1989, Rebecca Joseph, an applied anthropologist with experience in arts programming, folkarts, and community research, became the first director of the Connecticut Cultural Heritage Arts Program and the codirector of another program to promote the development of community artists referred to as the Inner City Cultural Development Program. Both programs continue at the ICR.

3. Other materials on the Brass Workers History Project include the Brass Workers History Project (1982) and Brecher (1984, 1986, 1988).

4. For my approach to oral history interviewing, as well as other aspects of community history, see Brecher (1985, 1996).

5. This documentary is distributed by Cinema Guild, New York, NY.

REFERENCES

Brass Workers History Project. (1982). Appendix: How this book was made. In J. Brecher, J. Lombardi, & J. Stackhouse (Comp. & Ed.), *Brass Valley: The story of working people's lives and struggles in an American industrial region.* Philadelphia: Temple University Press.

Brecher, J. (1984). How I learned to quit worrying and love community history: A pet outsider's report on the Brass Workers History Project. *Radical History Review, 28-30,* 187-201.

Brecher, J. (1985). Returning oral history to the community: A review of Cape Breton's magazine. *International Journal of Oral History, 6*(1), 63-67.

Brecher, J. (1986). A report on doing history from below: The Brass Workers History Project. In S. P. Benson, S. Brier, & R. Rosenzweig (Eds.), *Presenting the past: Essays on history and the public.* Philadelphia: Temple University Press.

Brecher, J. (1988). Doing history from below. In D. E. Moore & J. H. Morrison (Eds.), *Work, ethnicity, and oral history.* Halifax, Nova Scotia: International Education Center.

Brecher, J. (1996). *History from below: How to uncover and tell the story of your community, association, or union* (Rev. ed.). West Cornwall, CT: Commonwork/Advocate Press.

Brecher, J., & Costello, T. (Eds.). (1990). *Building bridges: The emerging grassroots: Coalition of labor and community.* New York: Monthly Review Press.

Glasser, R. (1995). *My music is my flag.* Berkeley: University of California Press.

Glasser, R. (1997). *Aqui me quedo.* Middletown, CT: Humanities Council.

Schensul, J. (1990). Organizing cultural diversity through the arts. In T. Carroll & J. Schensul (Eds.), Cultural diversity and the future of education: Visions of America [Special issue]. *Education and Urban Society, 22,* 377-392.

Serrell, B. (1996). *Exhibit labels: An interpretive approach.* Walnut Creek, CA: AltaMira.

Williamson, L. (1994). *Living legends: Connecticut master traditional artists* (Touring exhibition, catalogue, and video). Hartford, CT: Institute for Community Research.

Williamson, L. (1995). Sustaining cultural identities: Community arts in the U.S. In J. M. Fladmark (Ed.), *Sharing the earth: Local identity in global culture* (pp. 33-44). Aberdeen, Scotland: Robert Gordon University Press.

Williamson, L. (1996). *Auspicious signs: Tibetan arts in New England* (Exhibit, catalogue, and programming). Hartford, CT: Institute for Community Research.

Williamson, L., & Glasser, R. (1997). *Herencia Taina: Legacy and life* (Exhibit, brochure, and programming). Hartford, CT: Institute for Community Research.

SUGGESTED RESOURCES

Baron, R., & Spitzer, N. R. (1992). *Public folklore.* Washington, DC: Smithsonian Institution Press.

Schuldiner, D. (1993—). *Folklore in Use: Applications in the Real World.* Journal edited by David Schuldiner. Middlesex: Hisarlik Press. Twice yearly (June and December).

National Endowment for the Arts: Folk and Traditional Arts Program

This program provides national guidance in the development and persistence of folk and traditional arts programs in most states in the United States. It also provides specialized funding for infrastructure, special projects, exhibits and festivals, and apprenticeship programs. Telephone: (202) 682-5724; 682-5726; 682-5727. Website: http://arts.endow.gov (with links to many state folk arts programs and traditional arts initiatives).

American Folklife Center at the Library of Congress

This Center conducts research, provides national linkages and information, and holds national folkarts and folklife archives (script and text, photographs and other artifacts). Website: http://lcweb.loc.gov/folklife. Publication: *Folklife sourcebook: A directory of folklife resources in the United States and Canada* (1994).

Fund for Folk Culture

The Fund for Folk Culture is a privately supported foundation dedicated to the preservation, appreciation, dissemination, and study of the rich variety of folk cultures in the United States and abroad. P.O. Box 1566, Santa Fe, NM 87504-1566. Telephone: (505) 984-2534.

Practicing Anthropology

This is a quarterly publication of the Society for Applied Anthropology and a benefit of membership. It describes a wide variety of public programs, interventions, and other applications of ethnographic research. Society for Applied Anthropology, P.O. Box 24083, Oklahoma City, OK 73124.

INDEX

ABOUT THE AUTHORS, ARTISTS, AND EDITORS

Marlene Berg (M.U.P., New York University) is an urban planner grounded in community organization and urban economic development. For over a decade, she was responsible for evaluation and technical assistance to new organizations entering the United Way system in central Connecticut. One of the cofounders of the Institute for Community Research, she is currently Associate Director for Training, responsible for initiating and supporting national research demonstration and training projects at the Institute, including the Urban Women's Development Projects, the Rapid Socioeconomic Assessment Project, a participatory demographic study preceding the 1990 census, and the Inner City Cultural Development Program, an ongoing statewide training and development program for underserved urban artists. She currently directs a federally funded five-year demonstration study of substance abuse prevention for preadolescent girls. She has published on the status of Black Hartford, and the uses of ethnography in assessment, and wrote a 15-monograph series on the history and demography of neighborhoods and municipalities in the Hartford Capitol Region published by the ICR.

Jeremy Brecher, PhD, is a community-based historian in Connecticut, well known for his commitment to writing about and supporting projects that reflect history from the perspective of working people and community residents. He is the author of eight books, including *History From Below: How to Uncover and Tell the Story of Your Community Association or Union, Strike!, Building Bridges: The Emerging Grassroots Coalition of Labor and Community* coauthored with Tim Costello and *Brass Valley: The Story of Working People's Lives and Struggles in an American Industrial Region,* a compilation of material coauthored and coedited with Jerry Lombardi and Jan Stackhouse. He has written numerous papers on methods of conducting public history research with communities. His videos and other materials on the history of workers, African Americans, and Native peoples of Connecticut are widely used in schools and other educational institutions throughout the state and the Northeast.

Ruth Glasser, PhD, is a public historian and scholar with a community organizing background. She joined Jeremy Brecher as one member of a team committed to developing a series of radio programs and ethnic music festivals in Waterbury, Connecticut, as an outgrowth of community history. She has remained involved in both the production of educational materials on the music and culture of ethnic groups in the area and the production of scholarly works on Puerto Rican history and muscial traditions, including *My Music Is My Flag,* published by the University of California Press and *Aqui Me Quedo*, a history of Puerto Rican migration to Connecticut, published by the Connecticut Humanities Council. She consults to projects throughout the Northeast and New York on historical dimensions of public programs and exhibits, such as "Herencia Taina," a gallery exhibit on Taino cultural continuity, at the Institute for Community Research.

G. Alfred Hess, Jr., PhD, is a research professor in the School of Education and Social Policy at Northwestern University, where he also directs its Center for Urban School Policy. He has conducted more than 35 policy-oriented research projects on the Chicago Public Schools, and he has authored two books and edited a collection of school ethnographies. He was president of the Council on Anthropology and Education from 1996 to 1998. He currently directs a multidisciplinary longitudinal study of the redesign of 77 Chicago high schools that ranges from an analysis of achievement by 160,000 students to ethnographies of seven high schools where the staffs were reconstituted.

Margaret D. LeCompte is Professor of Education and Sociology in the School of Education at the University of Colorado at Boulder. After completing her MA and PhD at the University of Chicago, she taught at the University of Houston and the University of Cincinnati, with visiting appointments at the University of North Dakota and the Universidád de Monterrey, México. She also served as Executive Director for Research and Evaluation for the Houston Public Schools. In addition to her books, many articles, and book chapters, she co-wrote *Ethnography and Qualitative Design in Educational Research* and coedited *The Handbook of Qualitative Research in Education,* the first textbook and first handbook on ethnographic and qualitative methods in education. As a researcher, evaluator, and consultant to school districts, museums, and universities, she has published studies of dropouts, artistic and gifted students, school reform efforts, and the impact of strip mining on the social environment of rural communities. Fluent in Spanish, she is deeply interested in the education of language and ethnic minority children. She served as a Peace Corps volunteer in the Somali Republic from 1965 to 1967.

Ed Johnetta Miller is a weaver/silk painter/gallery curator/quilter and Master Teaching Artist. Her work has appeared in the *New York Times* and *FiberArts Magazine* and in the Renwick Gallery of the Smithsonian, American Crafts Museum, and Wadsworth Atheneum. She is the Director of OPUS, Inc., Co-Director of the Hartford Artisans Center, and consultant to Aid to Artisans, Ghana. She teaches workshops on weaving, silk painting and quilting to children and adults throughout the United States.

Bonnie K. Natasi, PhD, is Associate Professor and Director of the Programs in School Psychology at University at Albany, State University of New York. Formerly, she worked as a school psychologist in the New Orleans Public Schools. She has extensive experience in the use of videotape and audiotape for data collection and analysis. Her research and applied interests include the role of culture, school, and family in the promotion of mental health. She consults nationally and internationally with schools and communities regarding the development and evaluation of primary prevention programs. She coauthored a book titled *School Interventions for Children of Alcoholics.* She is Associate Editor of *School Psychology Review* and currently serves on the editorial boards of *Journal of School Psychology* and *Journal of Educational Psychology.*

Graciela Quiñones Rodriguez is a folk artist, carving *higueras* (gourds) and working in clay, wood, and lithographs with symbols and icons derived from Taino and other indigenous art forms. She builds *cuatros, tiples,* and other Puerto Rican folk instruments guided by the inspiration of her grandfather Lile and her uncle Nando who first introduced her to Puerto Rican cultural history and Taino culture and motifs. Her work has been exhibited in major galleries and universities thoughout Connecticut, at the Bridgeport Public Library, and at the Smithsonian Institute.

Jean J. Schensul is a medical/educational anthropologist. After completing her M.A. and Ph.D. at the University of Minnesota, she conducted intervention research in education at the Institute for Juvenile Research and Center for New Schools in Chicago. She served as co-founder and research director of the Hispanic Health Council in Hartford for ten years, and, since 1987, has been founder and executive director of the Institute for Community Research, based in Hartford, Connecticut, and dedicated to community-based partnership research. She has extensive experience in the use of ethnographic and survey research methods in the United States, Latin America, Southeast Asia, China, and West Africa. Her substantive interests are diverse, reflecting the contributions of ethnography to health, education, the arts, and community development. She coedited three special journal issues on applied research in education, and policy, and, with Don Stull, a book titled *Collaborative Research and Social Change: Applied Anthropology in Action,* and has published on other topics including substance abuse prevention, AIDS, adolescent development, chronic health problems, and the arts and community building. She is the recipient of a number of National Institute of Health Research grants, immediate past president of the Society for Applied Anthropology, former president of the Council on Anthropology and Education, and recipient (with Stephen Schensul) of the Kimball Award for Public Policy Research in Anthropology. She is adjunct professor of anthropology at the University of Connecticut and Senior Fellow, Department of Psychology, Yale University.

Lynne Williamson (M. Litt., University of Edinburgh) has been a museum professional for 21 years, receiving her training and the Museums Association Diploma of Great Britain at the Pitt Rivers Museum, University of Oxford. In the United States, she has held two curatorial positions, at the Native American Center for the Living Arts in Niagara Falls, and the American Indian Archaeological Institute in Washington, Connecticut, where she served as Project Coordinator for the National Endowment for the Humanities-funded exhibition *As We Tell Our Stories.* Based at the Institute for Community Research in Hartford since 1993, she directs the Connecticut Cultural Heritage Arts Program, a statewide folk arts initiative. Her work continues to involve professional museum practice, community-based oral history and technical assistance programs, arts administration, and research projects. She is of Mohawk-Mississauga descent; her father is a tribal member of Six Nations Reserve, Ontario. She serves as Adjunct Faculty at the University of Hartford, teaching "Native American Cultures."